TARIK TROTTER

You Name It

How to Experience Fulfillment In Every Area of Your Life While Being Contagiously Gold

First edition

ISBN: 978-1-7353523-0-5

Cover art by Ross Sampson

This book was professionally typeset on Reedsy.
Find out more at reedsy.com

This book is dedicated to Zechariah Elijah. Your passing away at the young age of nine years old, nine years ago, played an enormous role in the molding of the man I am becoming. All contributions I make to this world are an extension of the feeling I got when you looked into my eyes. I also dedicate this book to the human spirit. I am eternally grateful to the universe for allowing us an opportunity to be who we are. May this book be a contributing piece to our exploration of higher self.

self-help
self-improvement
self-investment

Ashley
Kimmy
Larynn
Khara

"*Mountains are the means. The man is the end. The goal is not to reach the top of the mountains, but to improve the man.*"

ARON RALSTON

Contents

Foreword

A word from Sean

I met Tarik in the summer of 2012 in New York City. At the time we were both in our early twenties and hungry to break into the music industry; he as an artist and myself on the management side. While I wasn't Tarik's manager early on, we would soon be spending a lot of time together in countless recording sessions and on different missions around the city, trying to scrap for opportunity and exposure.

Hip-hop is how we got to know each other, but we also bonded outside of music over a mutual craving for self improvement. We both devoured material about optimizing one's processes for organizing life, and reverse engineering the success of people we looked up to. We have a similar way of viewing the world in this regard, and we still share inspiring interviews and articles with each other regularly. One of my favorite anecdotes about Tarik came from a recommendation like this. We were recording a song in my apartment and I mentioned that he should check out a documentary I had recently watched about plant-based eating. In his calm, unassuming way, he took down the mental note and didn't say much about it. He may have asked me to text him the name of the movie later (it was *Forks Over Knives* for anyone interested), but that was it. About a month later, I casually asked him if he ever got a chance to check out that documentary. In the same modest way, he said that not only had he watched it, but he hadn't touched an animal product in weeks, and was now practicing a strict vegan diet. I remember being surprised by the response - this was a guy who publicly professed his love for McDonald's and would always join me on sandwich runs to the bodega. But four years later, he's turned a lesson on better diet choices into a lifestyle and even has the word "vegan" tattooed on his arm.

My hope is that readers can approach this book with the same open minded spirit and appetite for improvement that I've personally seen from Tarik on so many occasions such as this. He's someone who defied the status quo of his environment through a commitment to evolution and an embrace of change, even when it's uncomfortable. I find value in his point of view as a person with a wealth of unique, varied life experiences, who's also connected to the life-source of our culture, and understands how to package ideas in a way that feels current.

The intentions are pure and the message is authentic. Open yourself up to the contents of this book and I believe that there's a better you waiting on the other side.

Thank you for your years of friendship Tarik, it's an honor to be included.

-Sean Kane

A word from Evan

A special person is someone who lives each day with a purpose. Picasso said that the meaning of life is to find your gift, and that the purpose of life is to give it away.

Tarik is truly a *special* person, and "You Name It," is just one of MANY gifts Tarik is blessing the world with. Rarely do you find someone who has found their purpose at such an early age. You would think he's been on earth for a century now given how much knowledge and wisdom he brings to the table!

The older I become, the more I realize how valuable time is, and how important it is to devote time towards mental and spiritual growth. While there is a place for Netflix binging and Instagram scrolls, it's easy for me to get caught up in daily habits that steal time away from self-development. 'Mental naps', if you will.

Tarik challenges me to live intentionally, to think BIG and to live passionately and joyfully. I honestly don't even ask him how he's doing anymore because I know 'AMAZING' will always be his answer.

To Mr. Trotter:

- Thank you for waking up my mind and soul from doses of complacency.
- Thank you for managing to teach me something new every time we talk.
- Thank you for letting your 'highness' on life influence me in the most powerful of ways.

To the world:

- This book is going to wake you up and change your LIFE.
- Get ready for something *special*, and don't fall asleep!

\- Mr. Loo

A word from Yardley

~ The Honest Truth ~

Have you ever had someone come into your life and you feel an unmatched presence of love, happiness, honesty, and enthusiasm towards life?

My old man, whose death I will probably never "get over", told me that one day I will meet someone who meets all those qualities. Someone that will, no matter what, see people for their hearts and truly understand what it means to love.

As humans we spend too much time worrying about the unknown and the uncertainties of life. Tarik has shown me that those things do not matter, that everything in life is simple and why not "get over it" and be happy. Whether it is a broken heart, an injury, unemployment, or even death - it comes, and it goes. What matters is what you do with the time you have. Time is of the essence, and is the only currency of life; it is the only thing in life we do not get back, no matter how wealthy or great we are.

I remember the first day I met Tarik. We played basketball as though we had been long-time rivals. Not because we didn't like each other, but because we always had that competitive drive to bring the best out of one another. That first day was the start of something that many others can only dream of. It wasn't the start of a friendship, but the start of a brotherhood. A brotherhood that consisted of life in one of the many forms it takes. It was a connection that death itself can not take away. From literally sharing the same bed, to eventually living under the same roof, having moved across the country - we will continue to grow as one. We will continue to persevere and challenge ourselves because that's what brothers do.

This book will expose the hard work and dedication of Tarik. His words will truly impact your heart and soul. *"You Name it"* – Tarik has shown it and will continue to defy odds. His desire to make those around him happy, while feeling unconditional motivation is the reason he lives.

-Denzel Washington b.k.a. Yardley Marcelin

A word from Ross

Do you want to live a life full of regret?

If you've picked up this book and started reading, then it means you're searching for something. You might not know what it is or how to find it, but the important thing is that you're looking.

Spend 5 minutes talking to Tarik and you can feel the love he exudes towards everyone. His positivity is infectious and it's hard not to smile around him. He truly wants everyone to reach their true potential and find unique meaning in their lives.

But it's more than just enthusiasm. There's a deep caring that you feel when you talk to him. It's clear that he's put in the time, on himself, to face his own hardships, (and believe me, he's had them) and come out the other side an unstoppable force for positivity - he doesn't want to keep that for himself.

I personally I've talked with him when I've gone through some turbulent times in my life and the wisdom and insight he shares on how to work through them have been nothing short of spot on. The insights in this book will give you the tools to continually grow and build your inner strength and become the person you want to be. It's scary, I know - but I promise if you push past that fear and work through what this book has to offer, you'll be in a better place because of it. No doubt about it, you want Tarik in your corner.

-RJ Sampson

A word from Natalie

If you are lucky enough to know Tarik Trotter in real life, you know that his energy is special. He's a breath of fresh air, yet you feel like you've known him your whole life. He's a change-maker, someone who defies the odds, and he operates out of sheer love and gratitude. His mind is constantly creating, inventing, stretching, and writing, all while disrupting the status quo. He is one of the most selfless and benevolent human beings, and lives in a constant state of joy and admiration of other's strengths. Literally, everything he touches turns to gold. Because he is always in pursuit of the best version of himself, people around him naturally tend to get better too. Hang around him long enough and you will be brainwashed into believing you are infinite!

He didn't just magically become the way he is today. In fact, he has been dealt more bad hands than any one person deserves in a lifetime. You could say he attended the school of hard knocks, growing up in the inner city streets of New York. In *You Name It*, Tarik opens his heart and revisits some of the most heart-wrenching and traumatic moments from his upbringing, and just how they shaped the narrative of his life. Upon mastering himself, he was able to master peace (masterpiece). This rare honesty and vulnerability is extremely liberating for the reader, allowing you to fully lean into the book knowing you are in a safe space and will not be judged. This is not your traditional "self-help book". It's real, it's raw, and makes self-mastery more attainable and enjoyable. It feels like having a conversation with an old friend.

I've been so utterly blessed to witness this book come into fruition, and also see the remarkable man he became in the process of writing this into existence. Seemingly a walking magnet for miracles, he has poured his entire heart into these pages. His true purpose in life is to help others realize their infinite potential and unlock the highest versions of oneself.

We as a human race have the collective responsibility of leaving this world better than we found it, for our children and generations to come. The fact that you're holding this book in your hand is an incredible start. Make this copy your own—mark up the pages, write notes in the margins, highlight the one liners that resonate with you. Make this your work of art—literally, YOU NAME IT! Then pass it on to a friend. I also recommend listening to the audio book because of how candid, real, and passionate he gets when reading along.

Tarik, my love. You never cease to amaze me. You are the greatest gift and I am forever grateful. I am proud of you beyond words. The world will hear from you soon.

-Natalie "Nattymac" McKeehan

Preface

The date is December 2, 2019. Today was the first time that someone asked, "**What's the topic of your book**?" I'm not yet entirely sure why this question struck me so differently (that I did not have an immediate answer), being that I have been asked "What is your book about?" on many occasions leading up to this point– but addressing that head on and answering it here felt like a necessary thing to do.

One of the great struggles of my life has been trying to live amongst a society with norms that I was born to break. As I write this, I'm realizing that I was thrown off by this question because the day I decided that I was going to write this book, I wrote a list of what would be the **32** topics that I wanted to cover. So of course, it makes perfect sense that I was stumped when asked what the "topic" (without an 's' at the end) of my book was – the question was a bit of a box!

So, what is this book about? Well, *you name it*. Pun intended, yes, but I mean it – allow me to explain. The human spirit is far too complex for a one-sentence pitch. Instead of telling you what this book is about – because we would be here all day and I could probably write a book about what this book is about – I've placed a table of contents within these pages. So yeah, summing up this book will be left to you and what you take from it. I promise I'm not taking the lazy route and simply not choosing to explain because it's difficult to. It is more so just at the core of my intent to truly place the power of this book in YOUR hands.

Here is what I will say…

It is with the most humbling pleasure that I inform you of my purpose in this lifetime: to stretch what you know to be possible about your greatest capabilities, beyond what you currently know to be true, and as a result, bring out the very best in you. In order for you to unlock the gift of your full potential, there are steps that need to be taken, rules that need to be broken, beliefs that need to be expanded, and boundaries that must be walked beyond – but most importantly, a you IN YOU that needs to be challenged, broken, and ultimately pieced back together with tools that are made not just to last, but also molded to fit your forever-evolving spirit. Those tools lie right here, within the pages of this book.

Here is my ask of you...

Open your mind. Open your heart. Free your spirit. This book is a literary safe-haven for the person you are already becoming and will become while reading it. If you feel at all challenged by the words within the pages that follow – good. This book is not here to simply ride along with your current beliefs. It is not here to conform to, and color within the lines of the rules we have been taught. The ultimate take-away does not lie within these pages – **the ultimate take-away is the person you will become** after the completion of this book. Of course, I would love for you to apply what you learn here. That's a given. We will make that happen by your twisting every principle in this book into relatable form for yourself. Rather than take the examples used at face value, be sure to **extract the message behind the examples and spread them onto the areas of your life where they best fit**.

I hope you have fun with this. Growth ultimately turns into a form of self-love, when you really lean into it. Judge this book by how much more you grow to love yourself because of the life you create with the tools within these pages. Let's unlock doors within your being that rewrite everything we've been taught and know to be possible. Let's paint an even brighter future, starting with the canvas you have within yourself. No matter where you are now, I promise you that this book was written to get you to where you want to be.

I came back to write this paragraph on December 26th, 2019. I had to share with you some uneasy truths that I felt necessary to inform you about. Throughout the entirety of my writing this book, I have faced challenges outside of it. On this day, my bank account is currently -$235.84. That's a negative in case you missed it. It's been like that for the past 8 days or so, and that's nothing new. It had been even more in the negative a few times this year. My closest friends wouldn't know this. I definitely don't boast it. And I also do not carry myself like it. This year I learned about mentally, spiritually, and emotionally placing myself in shoes of a billionaire, long before the billions actually come. But why am I sharing this? Not to create a sob story. But so that you have proof to carry with you, always, that something beautiful and masterfully created can blossom even in the most challenging times. This book is that proof. I wrote it on days when I did not have any money to buy myself a meal during the day. I wrote this book when I did not have enough money to fly home for particularly important occasions of family and friends. I wrote this book when my car was getting towed due to a past due balance on my auto loan. The ENTIRE time, the part of me that remained and still remains unshaken was the very part that knew just how special what I have to share is. **No matter where you are in life right now, or what challenges lie in front of you and behind you, you still have 'SPECIAL' within you.** You are more than capable of blossoming out of a dark place.

It is now June 30, 2020. We are about 31 days from launch day, and I wanted to come back once more to share that my bank account is no longer in the negative. There are now thousands of dollars in it and growing. Writing this book forced me to stay true to the principles within these pages. All that is aligning in my life right now is a direct result of my application of what you will read here. And I can not wait for the transformation and manifestation that lies ahead for you as well.

If you're reading this, you are truly a blessing in my life, and more importantly one of the select incredible individuals who will tap into a version of yourself that majority of people have yet to even imagine. To be frank, most people have avoided the places within oneself that this book will take you to. For that reason and more, I am honored and thankful to have you join this journey with me. I am overwhelmingly excited to see just how far *you* take you. Enjoy. And be sure to share your experiences with me, and everyone you brush shoulders with. When you tap into the message in these pages, please spread it. Be contagiously-gold. Your capabilities are infinite.

With every ounce of love within me,

Tarik

Acknowledgement

I'm not entirely sure if anyone reads this, but I gotta say…thank you. I would firstly like to acknowledge the higher power that allowed for the writing of this book. Every up, down, high, low, and curve ball thrown at my life made for the words that were pieced together in the following chapters. I submit this work into the world, completely accepting of what may come from it. Secondly, I acknowledge you, the reader. Whatever or whoever it took to get you here, I deeply hope to propel you into an even further version of phenomenal being than you already are. Open your heart to the magic, and it will most certainly meet you halfway. Lastly, there are a few, okay I lied, a ton, of people I HAVE to thank for inspiring all that I am. Feel free to look up any of the following, and experience the great that they are.

God

My Family

Ross Jay Sampson

Natalie Mckeehan

Hal Elrod

Vishen Lakhiani

Jay Shetty

Tony Robbins

Will Smith

Kobe Bryant

Denzel Washington

Jorn Utzon

Nikola Tesla

Elon Musk

14th Dalai Lama

Desmond Tutu

Grant Cardone

Brandon Turner

Robert kiyosaki

Alfonso Gomez Rejon

Harriet Tubman

Sean Kane

Benjamin Klein

Sean Carter b.k.a. Jay-Z

Warren Buffet

Napoleon Hill

Oprah Winfrey

Serena Williams

Gary Vaynerchuk

Todd Morris

Mike Tyson

Kuczynska Maja

Tom Chi

Bill Gates

Michael Eleckert

Hayley Williams

Alex Banayan

Jada Pinkett Smith

Swizz Beatz

Ali Ramadan DHMHS

Banksy

Lebron James

Ace Hood

Sa-Roc

Keanu Reeves

Jim Carrey

Robin Williams

Aron Ralston

Alex Honnald

Jessica Meir

Christina Hammock Koch

Torre Washington

Nimai Delgado

Jidenna

Charlie "Rocket" Jabaley

Michael Phelps

Greta Thunberg

Arnold Schwarzenegger

Israel Adesanya

Connor McGregor

Chloe Coscarelli

Adele

Bruno Mars

Justin Timberlake

Timbaland

Tim Ferris

Jeff Provenzano

Verena Smit

Dani Tocci

Jamie Foxx

Martin Luther King Jr.

Biggs Burke

Justin "The Big Pygmy" Wren

Lewis Hamilton

Russell Westbrook

Jaden Smith

Leonardo Dicaprio

Marcus Kleveland

Jamie Anderson

Muhammad Ali

Maciek Jasik

Sasha Digiulian

Daniel Lau

Michael B. Jordan

Michael Jordan

Michael Jackson

1

Life is super hard. No, like really.

I t would absolutely take away from the transparency of this book if it failed to address reality. Optimism does not, by any means, speak to a lack of realism; it is a choice to seek out and acknowledge the good in anything that can be deemed *good or bad*. Optimism therefore is the acknowledgment of REAL experiences through a positive lens. Although life can be extremely difficult and trying, your lens is still YOURS. People may cloud it, circumstance may fog it, experiences may scratch it; but will you choose to see through that cloudy, foggy, and scratched up lens? Or will you fix it?

One of the most important distinctions that you can learn to make in this lifetime is the one between fault and responsibility. Not just the definitions, but the *distinction*. Fault is associated with things that have ALREADY occurred - things of the past - such as the actions of others and the choices that they have made. Responsi-**bility** is our a**bility** to control our responses. Ironically, the dictionary states that responsibility is having the "duty to deal with something." Whereas fault is defined as "misguided or dangerous action or habit."

You see where we are going with this, right? It's that accountability thing again. This time presenting itself in an even tougher pill to swallow. It is all too common and reasonable to focus on who or what is at fault when something happens – especially *to* us. But who or what is responsible for what we do about it? The answer demands a look in the mirror – which we will most certainly cover in a following chapter entitled *"How to face yourself"*.

I know someone who was molested as a child, on multiple occasions, by 4 older children and teens – boys and girls. Each time happening on weekends, which were supposed to be spent in safe arms, via a family-court order that was not consistently upheld. The molestation started from the age of 6 and went up to 11…not typically the ages when children let their parents know about these things – and so he didn't. Don't feel bad though. This child would later take that learned wrongful behavior and pass it on to younger kin very close to him up until his early teens. This child was me. And to be clear, I am saying that I did to others what was done to me, up until the age of 14 or so. This was a confusing and blurry time of life for me because I did not yet fully understand the effects of such things, they had never been explained to me, and I had not the slightest clue as to the impact that being molested could have on someone's life. So having a 13 year old girl ask me to pull down my pants when I was in the first grade was…unfamiliar.

It took decades before I was to learn the distinction between fault and responsibility. So for years I indulged in defaulting to a "this is my fault" *internal dialogue*, and a lack of forgiveness for myself and for the people who hurt me. I even held a grudge toward the person who was supposed to take care of me on weekends, thinking that… had this person done what they were supposed to, I would have never been molested. Most importantly and detrimentally, I held a grudge against myself for harming others. To be completely transparent with you, there were recently still days when this internal frustration arose – but thankfully the practice of facing myself and my fears have allowed room for **the ability to let go of thoughts and feelings that no longer serve** me.

It was not until almost 20 years after first experiencing this, that I realized and learned how much dwelling and holding on to on my past would ultimately bring me down and hold me back. I was slapped in the face with a harsh reality – that being… there was no changing my past, and that I now had a *responsibility* to channel something good from it. And in regard to forgiving myself, I had to accept that this was not my *fault*. There is no room for fault. **The quest for fault leads to external circumstances that require internal addressing.** It very well could be someone's else fault for what happened to me as a child, but it became my **responsibility** to deal with it head-on.

My childhood never got any easier. I would go on to experience an actual famine in my household by the age of nine. I knew what an eviction was before learning multiplication. I witnessed murder before going to middle school. All while hiding a dark secret from everyone I knew. I still had no entitlement to an excuse, nor hall pass from responsibility.

It VERY WELL may be someone else's fault for things that have occurred in your life. **You STILL have a *responsibility* and duty to seek out and find the good in it, or the good that you can do because of it.** If you do not want to do this, seek out the alternative and see how far It gets you; I've tried. I share these things with you because it took me years to find and grasp the power that I actually have, which is fueled by my responsibility; and I'm hoping to help you find your power way sooner.

If you have been broken, you have a responsibility to pull yourself together; even if it wasn't your fault. In the midst of pulling yourself together, you will lift weights you never thought possible. Rather than seeking an imaginary "easier" time in our lives, we can be more effective and PROactive by simply growing to match the capacity of our responsibilities. Life truly can be brutal at times, but if the alternative to finding good in everything is…folding, then I will blindly chase every ounce of positivity I possibly can. We all should.

I also *do not* regret to inform you that once you are aware of your responsibility, fault is no longer a valid excuse. This is tough because **the fact that you don't always place yourself where you end up, is an easy and truthful way out of facing yourself. But it is equally as much a choice as it is truth.** Most of the time, we are already smart enough to identify a change that we must make, but we won't because it's uncomfortable. Now, if life is already giving you a hard time, and clearly trying to communicate a necessary shift in your being, yet you're still choosing to resist it… you will continue to manifest a repeat of the same lesson in different forms. This is not cool. We experience this in relationships, finances, workplaces, our bodies, goals, and more.

There are real things happening in your life, and that is not to be downplayed nor discounted. No matter where you are, or wherever you've come from to get *here*, you're experiencing or have experienced a system/environment of some sort. Some systems and environments are extremely difficult to overcome; others have more breathing room for flourishing. Neither of these are in your control, and the former will present a hell of a lot more reason to give up… on everything. When at the point of feeling as though your best option is to give up, there is no secret ingredient to escaping that. It's just you and choice. And this is why *affirmations* (we'll dive into this later) are so crucial – because motivation is never there when you actually need it. It's there when you're searching for a YouTube video to get you going. It's there when the right people doing the right things are around you. It's there when you're seeing results and manifesting success. But when you are down, like really down…motivation is absent. Motivation does not present itself in times like these because it requires **YOU as a <u>thriving</u>** vessel.

We have to stop wishing and looking for our situations to change or be "better". YOU have to breathe life into yourself. YOU have to gas yourself up. YOU have to break the wall that your back is against. And in case you missed what was mentioned a moment ago...motivation needs YOU, not the other way around. Nothing good may present itself and be accepted, by a person who has not mentally, spiritually, physically, or emotionally positioned themselves to receive it. In the following chapters, we will push this conversation forward by discussing *how* to position ourselves in a way that allows us to experience a whole-fulfilled experience of the <u>good</u> that life has to offer – the very good that we deserve – because if there is one thing I have learned from ~~going~~ growing through the most trying times of my life, it's that **our capabilities are infinitely fueled**, not limited, **by our circumstances**. If you don't believe that now, you will by the end of this book.

IF YOU HAVE
BEEN BROKEN,
YOU HAVE A
RESPONSIBILITY
TO PULL
YOURSELF
TOGETHER; EVEN
IF IT WASN'T
YOUR FAULT.

2

Brainwash Yourself 101

For the purpose of this particular book, the term "brainwash" is going to take on a bit of a new meaning. In these pages, it refers to the effect that the tiniest, most subtle, and seemingly harmless words, actions, programs, and thought processes have on us. I'm mostly composed and peaceful; although I occasionally get emotionally charged at the thought of the carelessness I've seen most people walk around with in regard to what you're about to read. Here's a specific example: people don't consider it to be a big deal if you say something like "my stamina is terrible" in response to someone asking you to go on a hike or play sports. (Let this book serve as a means to an end - the exorcism and annihilation of words that serve you no good!) The only thing those words do in this scenario is further separate you from a truth that the more lax side of you may not want to face. The truth is not that your stamina is terrible (at least not to this brainwashed mind). *The truth is that your stamina needs work and development!*

I get how minuscule of a difference this is – but what if I told you that the effect could be... life-changing? Saying something like this once may very well be harmless indeed, but over the course of time, sayings like these become detrimental *affirmations* (which are things repeated that your mind believe to be true, and we'll get to the importance of this). And I've got just the interesting example to prove it...

Before a plane takes off, it has a flight plan. That flight plan factors in things like weather and wind. Based on those conditions, the plane is given a flight plan that must be adhered to, in order to get to its destination safely. Say this plane goes 2 degrees off course – it's only 2 degrees, right?

Well, no. According to a former Air Force pilot, every 1 degree off course means a plane will miss its destination by 92ft per mile.

1° off course = 92ft per mile from the destination

2° off course = 184ft per mile from the destination

If you haven't already, allow me to put this in perspective. If a plane flies 3,000 miles, say from New York City to Los Angeles, and is 2 degrees off course – it would miss the LAX airport by 552,000 ft... aka 104 miles! That could be the difference between land and the middle of the ocean. For those of us who can use some strengthening in math because its just hasn't been our thing, I apologize for taking you through aviation school a moment ago. Notice however, that I did not say "for those of us with weak math skills". (That would be a terrible *affirmation*)

The point here is that "little things" sum up to *very big things* over time if they are not watched and handled with intent – our words fall within the lines of this principal. So after saying "I'm not a morning person" for a year, you'll be *THAT much farther* (*2° off course*) from being energized in the mornings (your destination)! A small switch to "I am becoming the kind of person who is energized in the mornings" can make all the difference.

I once learned a story of a person diagnosed with short-term memory loss as a result of a head-on car collision with a drunk driver. Damage done to his brain was so fatal that simple tasks on the job were no longer plausible or doable responsibilities. If someone were to ask something of him, he would tell them that he's not the guy for the job. Even if what was asked was something so small as dropping an envelope in the mail 30 minutes later. He went months like this; turning down any thing asked of him that would require his memory. (I genuinely wish that I had an immediately life-impacting, mind-blowing ending to this story. Instead I'll tell you the truth.) What's interesting here is that this man adopted the harsh reality of his circumstance; so much so, that he would no longer even *try* to remember things. He was convinced that the effect of his accident was so permanent a crutch, that he would just *have to* live with it. Doctors stating that he would never fully regain his memory weren't exactly confidence boosters either. It took getting fed up with his current state, to get to the point where he decided that just telling himself "My brain is capable of healing itself and my memory can improve" was at least worth a try. He did this every day for a few weeks, and what would come of it is a moment where his subconscious took over and answered a question for him.

"Would you mind taking this downstairs when you leave?" Someone asked.

Almost immediately, *he replied "Sure thing."*

This man is Hal Elrod, author of *The Miracle Morning*, and one of my closest friends. He probably wouldn't call me one of his closest friends – and I'll explain what I mean by that in a later chapter titled *"How to change your group of friends."* For now, note that **Hal changed something within himself that even the most expert of doctors deemed improbable.** He could remember again. Take a moment to visually grab hold of the kind of mindset and belief in oneself required, to go from diagnosed, to medical anomaly.

Hal states *"Our programming is a result of...what we have been told by others, what we have told ourselves, and all of our life experiences...We must stop programming ourselves for a life of mediocrity by focusing on what we're doing wrong, being too hard on ourselves when we make mistakes, and*

causing ourselves to feel guilty, inadequate, and undeserving of the success we really want." Credit: *The Miracle Morning: The Not-So-Obvious Secret Guaranteed to Transform Your Life (Before 8am) by Hal Elrod*
I'm not sure about you, but I read that and translate it something along the lines of…**nothing that anyone states to me, nor anything that has happened in my past deserves to have more of a say in who I am becoming, than me myself. If this is true, then it is best that I be careful and methodical with anything that plays a role in my mental, emotional, spiritual, and physical programming. The mind can be brainwashed. Just change the program.**

Becoming aware of this truth is the first step on the ladder to your higher self. Most of our fears and thinking patterns were not formed by us, but rather by external circumstance – our environment, experiences, schooling, news, social media, etc. Brainwashing ourselves can be as simple as flipping on our awareness switch. Rather than allow ourselves to unconsciously and unintentionally consume whatever is placed in front of us, let's start by making a conscious & intentional decision to seek out, acquire, and digest all the good that the universe has for us.

Here are some questions we never ask ourselves…

- *How can we turn a 4-hour Netflix binge into bettering ourselves?*
- *How much of the 2 hours spent on Instagram today visually inspired us to take the kind of action that brings us closer to the life of our dreams?*
- *What return on investment are we seeking from happy hour this Friday? Does it add value to our lives?*
- *How do our plans with friends later today bring us all closer to breaking through?*
- *What is the food I'm eating right now doing to my body short-term and long-term?*
- *How is this movie/tv show helping me leave with new perspective that I*

can apply to my biggest dreams?
- *How is this dating app making me a better version of myself for the relationship I hope to have?*

Questions like these can definitely come off as judge-y, but I promise the point is simply to put us in a place where we can diagnose the programming of our subconscious mind - the part of our brains that are on auto-pilot. Questioning all that we do allows us to see what we can tweak in our lives to become better versions of self. We can actually watch movies that make us smarter, read books that raise our vibrations, binge watch shows that inspire and bring light to areas of our lives that need work, hang around people who challenge us to think and grow richer, use apps to actually make connections that add value rather than just watch what other people are doing, and eat foods that give our bodies life - all in addition to letting loose, having fun, and doing whatever we want to do as well. I'm not saying let's be mundane robots who don't enjoy entertainment; I'm saying **the starting point for brainwashing ourselves to be greater lies in questioning everything we do, for the sake of growing more aware**. This was *Brainwash Yourself 101* - let's up things a bit in the chapters ahead.

RATHER THAN ALLOW OURSELVES TO UNCONSCIOUSLY AND UNINTENTIONALLY CONSUME WHATEVER IS PLACED IN FRONT OF US, LET'S START BY MAKING A CONSCIOUS + INTENTIONAL DECISION TO SEEK OUT, ACQUIRE, AND DIGEST ALL THE GOOD THAT THE UNIVERSE HAS FOR US.

3

How to change your mindset

This chapter may be one of the most important. And I may say that about every chapter, but don't let that decrease the significance of this one. As a matter of fact, I'd say that this chapter plays the most significant part in allowing you to be open and receptive to all that follows. To be completely transparent with you, I stumbled upon this by getting fed up with hearing it from people.....who did not explain HOW.

You're familiar with the conversation right? It goes something like...

You: *"I feel kind of stuck. I know there's more out there for me, but I'm having trouble getting there..."*

Guru: *"Well the first thing you need to do is change your mindset."*

You: **Ok, great. Let me go get started on that with all I just learned.**

3 hours later: **Realizes nothing was learned**.... **maybe closes eyes really hard and tries to change the way your mind works on the spot** .... **fails**

Then, repeat a couple of months later.

This might not be EXACTLY how it does down, but you get the gist. We've all heard the saying. So I'll get right to it. I did think about dragging it out a tad longer like a guru who wants your credit card would, but luckily for you, I'm legitimately gung-ho on adding value to your life and desire nothing in return. Actually that's a lie. I do want something in return: for you to APPLY this staring right now. It's the only way that this works. I'm dragging this out, aren't I? Okay, here we go...

The best way for me to go about this is to show you the order in which most people operate throughout the entirety of their lives; followed by what we all should ACTUALLY be doing. The key here is the order in which following processes take place. Diagram time...

What most people are doing

1. **Life** (happens)

2. **Internal Dialogue** (what we tell ourselves about our experiences)

3. **Mindset** (what we think and believe about our circumstances)

4. **Actions** (we take...more like REactions)

What we should be doing

1. **Internal Dialogue** (Talk to yourself)

2. **Mindset** (we believe what we tell ourselves)

3. **Action** (We do what we believe we can)

4. **Life** (A reflection and byproduct of what we do)

Diagram 1

I know, I know. There's a lot of gray area up there. However, I recently learned that gray area is actually just made up of black and white; so let's dive in and clarify both sides. Note that both sequences of *diagram 1* list *internal dialogue* immediately before *mindset*. It's also important to note where "Life" is sequenced in each - in the former, we can only react because *Life* happens prior to our deciding what we will make of it. As for the latter, we have already decided what *Life* will be. Although uncontrollable things will occur, the order in which we choose to operate remains very much in our hands.

What Most People Are Doing

This part really pains my heart. I see it happening on a day to basis. People living half-fulfilled lives, no where even close to tapping into their full potential; genuinely wanting more, but doing nothing more than reacting to everything that happens to them. This is your classic "proactive vs. reactive" situation. But I'm going to open this up in a way that you most definitely have not heard, seen, or read before.

Part 1 - Life

Life happens. What I mean here is an impacting event, or period of time spent going through something(s), or period of time spent in a certain physical, mental, spiritual, or emotional state. Here are a few examples: a loss of some sort – maybe a family member, maybe a house, or money, or simply an opportunity; failing a test, failing at a business you started, didn't make the team, suffered an injury, everyone forgot about you, a really bad break up, financial debt, getting fired, getting jumped, shot, physically abused, sexually abused, mentally and emotionally abused, cheated on, neglected, depressed, working a job you don't want to be at, in a relationship you don't want to be in, growing up in a rough neighborhood, extremely difficult childhood, feeling/being stuck, parents weren't there for you, no one believes in you, no one listens to you, no one understands you, no doors are opening up, you got *here* but have been unable to get *there*, and you just keep getting slapped in the face with a bunch of everything you did not ask for and probably do not deserve. If you have ever experienced any of these things, place your hand on your chest right now, and take a moment to express thankfulness that your heart is still beating and that you are alive enough to be reading the words that are about to follow.

Part 2 - Internal dialogue

This is a fancy and more socially acceptable way of saying that we talk to ourselves. Don't feel attacked – everyone is doing it. This is the mental chatter that we have going on in our heads throughout the day; the voice that no one hears, except you – and interestingly enough, *half the time the voice isn't even you* (but I'll get to that in a bit). After *part 1* has taken place, now is the time where the most detrimental of these 4 steps get to work. We tell ourselves things, that further confirm and manifest a continuation of what is already happening. We'll say things to ourselves, such the following...

HOW TO CHANGE YOUR MINDSET

"I really don't feel like getting out of bed this morning"

"This sucks"

"I really don't want to be here today"

"I just wanna go home"

"I can't deal with this right now"

"I can't trust him/her"

"I can't figure this out"

"I can't talk"

"I'm not good at that"

"I don't feel like doing this"

"It's fine, it's just this once"

"Literally nothing is going my way"

"I can't catch a break"

"I'm going to fail this test"

"That is not my strength"

"I don't have the time"

"There's not enough time"

"There's nothing I can do"

"It doesn't really matter"

"I'll workout later or tomorrow"

"I don't care anymore"

"I'm alone"

"I hate myself"

"I wish I had"

"I wish I could"

"They don't appreciate me"

"It probably wouldn't have worked anyways"

"I have so much to do"

"I don't like my body/nose/hips/etc"

"I'm ugly"

"What I think/say/do doesn't matter"

"I'm okay with just this"

"I'll never be rich"

"I'm a burden to others"

"Nothing is going to change"

"That's way too early for me"

"This just isn't for me"

"I'm not a morning person"

"I already tried that"

"I could never do that"

"I'm stuck"

"I suck at that"

"I'm not good enough"

"No one likes me"

"I'm depressed"

"This isn't going to work"

"I'm not smart enough"

"This is too much for me"

"I can't even"

"I can't"

"I'm stressed"

"My anxiety is too much right now"

"I can't be here"

"It's too late for me"

"I have the worst luck"

"I'm not in his/her league"

"No way"

"It's too hard"

"I could never be like him/her"

"I'll do it later"

"They don't like me"

"This always happens to me"

"Great, now my whole day is ruined"

"That's impossible"

"I look horrible today"

"This is the worst"

"I screw everything up"

"Love is not for me"

"I'm not strong enough"

"I shouldn't talk about my feelings"

Diagram 2

17

This is just a glimpse of our day to day self-talk. By the time you finish this chapter – no longer will these kinds of phrases be acceptable. They may not seem like a big deal, but what's happening as you repeat them is astounding. You're actually putting together a jingle, and life is absolutely going to play along! This is the part where you must ask yourself…what & who's song are you singing?

If McDonald's were to sing "Ba da bah bahh bahhh…" – you would know to sing "I'm lovin' it".

If Peyton Manning were to sing "Nationnnn widee is onnnnn…." – you would know to sing "your sideeee".

If someone were to sing "The bestttt part of wakinggg upp…" – you would probably know to sing "is Folgers in yourrr cuppp!"

The point here is that we know the songs of billion-dollar corporations that don't care about us in the slightest bit – due to repetition. You've simply heard them enough. Therefore, it is safe to say that if something is heard or repeated frequently enough, we grow to learn it and know it by heart. **Imagine then, how detrimental…or instrumental…your *own* jingle can be.** Which of the statements in *diagram 2* have you been repeating to yourself? (for long enough that you could run a million-dollar ad campaign and be completely sold!) If we are naturally sold on our own *internal dialogue* (aka jingles), then we better make sure that starting right now, we are 100% conscious of what we are saying, until we subconsciously know it as well as we know the McDonald's jingle.

Part 3 -Mindset

Our minds become _set_ on things we tell ourselves over and over again. We mentally accept *parts 1 and 2*, knowing deep down that something is off. We're now at the point where our thoughts are so deeply rooted, that we justify the actions that follow. We're gearing up our *reactions* (because that's what we do when life is happening *TO* us). We are _set_ on no one deserving to be let in, we are set on not being able to talk to anyone, our mind is set on not opening up, set on believing this is now our worth, set on believing we'll relive the same experiences again, set on life being this way, set on not speaking or reaching out, set on no longer having high hopes or dreams, set on most sayings in life just being clichés that hold no real value, and set on our new truth – which is that this is the way things are and we'll just have to accept it and make the most of what's happening. The danger here is that **when our minds are _set_ on something, that is what we BELIEVE, and our ACTIONS mirror what we believe. Mindset means practically immovable, incapable of being adjusted, not open to outside possibilities, and automatically in disagreement with anything that does not confirm the current bias**. If you have ever been here, or still are – it's extremely difficult to admit to it. Stubbornness can be a strength, but consider how weak and vulnerable it can leave you if misplaced.

Part 4 - Action

We act a certain way. Let's just call it what it is and admit that we *react*. Once life happens, here is what we do: we become closed off, we are emotionally inaccessible or unavailable, we stop trusting (even ourselves), we don't try again, we don't try as hard, we stop believing, we replace 'optimistic' with 'realistic', we hurt others with the hurt that we have learned, we shut down, we bounce back temporarily then lose motivation, we never love as hard, we become afraid, we project our experiences on people and/or children with dreams, we harden our hearts and minds, we collapse, we turn to things we know damn well we shouldn't, we take steps backwards, we go through the motions just to go through the motions, we do drugs, we drink, we numb ourselves, we hang around people who haven't identified with themselves, we stop speaking, we don't reach out, we don't ask for help, we stop knocking, we spend time and money on more on things that yield no emotional or mental or spiritual return on investment, we choose not to recover because we don't want to experience again, we worsen our habits, we indulge in bad habits, we snooze the alarm more, we transfer this new dead energy we're carrying onto people around us or people we sleep with or people we're in relationships with, and we find every reason we can to suck the life out of any potentially-good thing because we are selfishly still holding on to something we experienced in the past. We are *subconsciously or consciously* slave to what's happened. Again… If you have ever been here, place your hand on your chest right now, and take a moment to express thankfulness that your heart is still beating and that you are alive enough to be reading/hearing the words that are about to follow.

Let's flip the order of these 4 steps, and reveal **how to change our mindset.**

What We Should Be Doing

Note: The following is a method to creating the life that you have been wanting. Yes, this is a proven method. I'm living proof, and I have learned it from even more efficient and successful living proofs before me. Keep this close to heart.

Part 1 - Talk to yourself

Now yes, it's true that we already do this. But in what order? Typically we do this too late, and based on things that happen prior - talking to ourselves in a <u>reactive</u> state. When we switch the order of this step to our first, we dictate the mood of the conversation life is having – and THIS changes EVERYTHING. This brings out the pro in PROactive.

Here's what the internal dialogue of an ultra-lit & incredible human looks like.

"I am amazing."

"I am incredible."

"I am unstoppable."

"My past only catapults me into a better version of who I am today"

"I can do this"

"I will figure this out"

"I am happy to be here"

"I am working on getting where I want to be"

"I am creating the life of my dreams."

"Somehow, this will be better for me in the future"

"I can trust again"

"I can love again"

"This is bigger than me"

"I am not alone"

"I will change my current situation to one more desirable"

"I am in charge of my life"

"Although outcomes are uncontrollable, I control my actions"

"I put out good energy, I receive good energy."

"I am capable"

"I create time to do the things I need to"

"I am intentional about making time"

"I am deserving of true love"

"I am deserving of a healthy relationship"

"I can pass this test"

"I can launch this business successfully"

"I am capable of handling any circumstance"

"Every obstacle builds me up"

"Pain only builds my character"

"I can take risks"

"Stress is just proof that I am capable"

"I am choosing to do better today"

"I'm going to get it done now"

"I can push through this"

"I will thank myself for this later"

"It's possible"

"I am stronger than my anxiety"

"I constantly bounce back"

"4 hours is more than enough sleep"

"I am a staple in this universe"

"Life is on my side"

"This is making me stronger"

"I can and will crawl myself out of this state"

"There is more for me right here."

"I'm super attractive"

"I am creative"

"I win"

"Realistically, I will remain optimistic"

"I am unshaken"

"I am unbroken"

"I am not a burden to my friends or people"

"I can reach out for help"

"I get better by the minute"

"I can overcome this"

"I am magical"

"This is the best thing that could have happened"

"I will grow to better understand this"

"This is bigger than me"

"I have the power to change this"

"Good or bad, who knows? I am still positive"

"I am growing stronger"

"I am growing better"

"I add value to everything and everyone I touch"

"I am loved"

"I am appreciated"

"I am valued"

"I mean something"

"I am here for a reason"

"I'm a great listener"

"I'm great at making connections"

"Failure does not mean quit"

"I love myself"

"I'm obsessed with myself"

"My imperfections are perfect for me"

"I impress myself often"

"I can have anything that I want"

"I will get out what I put in"

Diagram 3

22

Now, applying the principal of repetition that we discussed previously, imagine the affect these kinds of words have on a person's mindset. Imagine the jingle playing in this person's mind on a day to day basis. And imagine what happens when this person learns these words just as well, if not better, than they know Kit Kat's jingle or the alphabet song.

Part 2 - Minset

When words like the ones above are consistently repeated internally, the mind begins to expand what it knows to be true about current circumstance and possibilities. The mind then becomes _set_ on having no limits, set on winning, set on creating, set on adapting, set on action, set on positivity, and set on understanding that no matter the circumstance, the only way to come out is a better version of self. This kind of mindset speaks to *capability*, whereas the previous and most common mindset speaks to inability.

If the person who believes they can, and the person who believes they can't are both the same... it's important for us to ask ourselves - which person are we? Because each mindset is directly correlated to the actions taken by that person.

Simply put, you will do 1 of 2 things:

1) Believe that you are unable, and act as such.

2) Believe that you are able, and act as such.

To ensure that we are on the same page here, what I am stating is that **if the mind believes and knows to be true, anything repeated to it, then you can and WILL change your mindset by FIRST changing what is repeated to it**. Nothing is repeated more to the mind, than what we are *saying to ourselves* on a day to day basis. When we *START* by talking to ourselves, we set the tone for the narrative, our minds eventually believe what is being told and communicated to them, and because of that – we will now act on those beliefs. Life then responds to and reflects our actions.

To make this practical, allow me to tell the story of 'the alarm clock theory':

Rachel goes to bed later than expected. 12:00am. **Life**

She's communicated to herself that this is too late. **Internal Dialouge**

She also believes anything less than 8 hours of sleep is not enough and she is not going to be well-rested. **Mindset**

Rachel's alarm clock goes off at 5:00am (the time she actually wants to get up)...

Knowing that she has back-up alarms set to go off and "10 more minutes won't hurt"...

Rachel hits the snooze button. **Action**

Rachel snoozes 5 more times. («this is the action she is taking based on her belief and what she has told herself)

Rachel finally gets out of bed and now feels behind and rushed to get to work/school on time. "Life" repeats.

The internal dialogue she is now having most likely sounds like *"I really don't feel like getting in today"* or *"I'll workout later, there's not enough time now"* etc. Thus reinforcing her being the kind of person that does not create the life she wants, and **manifesting a repeat experience** of not getting the things she wants out of life. To show you exactly where the opportunity to apply the more efficient order of operating lies, let's look at the same story, this time changing the sequence in which we go about the 4 steps...

Jasmine goes to bed later than expected. 12:00am

Jasmine communicates to herself that this has happened before, and that she is fully capable of functioning at a high capacity off 5 restful hours of sleep. **INTERNAL DIALOGUE**

Jasmine's alarm clock goes off at 5:00am...

Although tired, she does not snooze. She believes she is capable of functioning exceedingly well from 5 restful hours of sleep... **MINDSET**

Jasmine gets out of bed off 1 alarm. **ACTION**

Jasmine gets to the gym, does her morning routine un-rushed, and gets to work/school with plenty of time to spare. **LIFE**

I believe it goes without saying how life responds to Jasmine, because that's the exact kind of morning we would probably all opt for in an ideal world. No one enjoys snoozing multiple times. We enjoy the extra sleep, yes, but not the action of being woken up over and over and over again to a loud sound. No one likes *not* having the kind of morning that you intended to. And no one likes feeling or being rushed. Most importantly, no one likes the kind of life that is created from doing these things repeatedly each day. You'll never get to the gym! Not enough to get the results you want.

You more than likely noticed that the order of the story stayed the same, but we **manually made changes to how we respond** to what's happening. This is incredibly important because that small change, has a big effect on the outcome. In this example, it greatly altered the outcome of the type of morning Rachel and Jasmine had. Imagine the effect these 4 steps have over the course of a week, a few months, or even 1-5-10 years! Both stories began with a very realistic and sometimes uncontrollable - getting to bed later than expected. The decisions made at 12:00am were the only difference. An uncontrollable circumstance does not have to be the starting point. **Choose your starting point by having an ongoing conversation with self that does not move its place in line when faced with circumstance.** No matter where you are, start with internal dialogue, and your mind will follow.

Part 3 - Action

The stories within this chapter are perfect examples of how our actions tend to follow our mindsets. Whether intentionally or unintentionally, the way we act and the things we do on a day to day basis ultimately shine light on the condition of our minds. The same goes for the things we *don't* do or *don't* act upon. If you have not launched the business you've been thinking about, that shows that your mind may be set on your needing more money before you can, or your being afraid to fail, or your thinking you won't succeed, or your being concerned about what others will think or say. If someone hasn't read the book you recommended, that shows that their mind may be set on believing they don't have enough time, or that "next week" they'll have more time, or that they're not really much of a reader. If you're reading this right now, that shows that *your mind is set* on there potentially being something within these pages that will add value to you. At the end of the day, we will either **act** on what we believe, or choose **not to act** based on what we believe.

Part 4 - Life

I don't want to overcomplicate this - your life is currently your holding a book that is adding value to your life. This is a direct result of an action you took; that action being opening the damn thing. Just like this action you took to get here, **every single thing that you can imagine and desire out of this life are just *actions* away. Now that you know your actions are taken (or not taken) based on what your <u>mind is set</u> on, and you also now know that your mind is set on the things you constantly repeat to yourself - you understand that YOU ARE RESPONSIBLE for changing your life, YOU CAN change your life, and YOUR LIFE IS A REFLECTION OF YOU and these 4 steps**. Talk (insert clap). To (insert clap). Yourself (insert clap). First (insert clap).

Strip this chapter down to its most basic form and you will find that we can change our mindset by first changing the way that we talk to ourselves. If you have any doubt whatsoever that life, and our experience of it, is a byproduct of our mindset – then I encourage, and double-dog dare you to try changing your internal dialogue. This practice is of course ineffective without the same level of consistency in which we hear billion-dollar companies shove their ad campaigns and catchy jingles into our ears. So do it consistently! It's gotta be an every day thing, *or your default self-talk will take over*. We've got an entire chapter on consistency in the pages ahead. Feel free to skip forward if you'd like. And in case you were wondering, we most definitely will tap into how to apply the art of talking to yourself. Which leads me to our next topic – *Affirmations*.

IF THE MIND BELIEVES
AND KNOWS TO BE
TRUE, ANYTHING
REPEATED TO IT, THEN
YOU CAN AND WILL
CHANGE YOUR MINDSET
BY FIRST CHANGING
WHAT IS REPEATED TO
IT..

4

Do You Even Affirmation Bro? Sis?

I'll start this off by clearly and simply explaining what an affirmation is: ***Anything* that you repeat to yourself over and over until the point of knowing it to be true.** I imagine that you're moreso familiar with the popularly known take on affirmations being really positive things that you say to yourself about what you want from life. The issue is that 1) not many people are doing that enough, and 2) it doesn't *have to be positive* to qualify as an affirmation. ***Anything*** that we tell ourselves repetitively will most certainly fill the role. Which is why, for the most part, the only things being affirmed are our internal dialogue around our current situation, and what we feel about life as it happens "*to*" us.

While we are here, allow me to rip what is in the above quotations apart – for good. Life does not happen "to" us. Life happens *for* the person we are becoming. There is not one bit of accountability in stating that something has happened or is happening "to" us – all that does is make for an easy out. However, when you state that something is happening or has happened *FOR* the person you are becoming, it implies that there is a reason which you may or may not fully understand – but requires you to set aside any *fault,* and accept your responsibility to explore the "why." Stop. Avoiding. This.

It is selfish to immediately make every circumstance or situation about you. The future you would really appreciate if you handed forward some knowledge and growth from your current experiences; this way that very knowledge and growth can be applied to your future experiences, and repeat.

We can all think of at least one thing from our past that really sucked at the time – maybe even broke us. But looking back now, we are somewhat thankful that it happened, and maybe even made us better. If this is true, what makes any current situation different?

If you don't have something like that from your past, then you most certainly do have this fact: **you are 100% undefeated**. I would not be surprised to find that you're questioning my sanity right now, so please allow me to explain: If you are currently reading this book, then you are, in fact, still alive. If you are still alive, then you have gotten through 100% of your worst days and times. And **if you have gotten through or are still going through 100% of your worst days and times, then you are by definition – undefeated**.

To be clear, the definition of "defeat" is to be demoralized and overcome by adversity. We have not been <u>overcome</u> by adversity; we've <u>grown through</u> it. Please say the following aloud and as though you know it to be true: I AM 100% UNDEFEATED.

(Now *that's* an affirmation. And it segments perfectly into my getting back on track...)

At all times, we are all affirming *something*. This can be via our thoughts, internal dialogue, or things we say aloud. One of the most common ways this truth presents itself is on Sunday evening when we either say or think to ourselves something along the lines of "tomorrow is going to suck" or "I don't feel like going to (*you name it*) tomorrow". Trust me when I say that life will reflect those words, because your actions will align with them. You have affirmed the kind of Monday you're going to have.

What's my point? Well, if you have stated words similar to the ones in the above Sunday evening example, whether internally or aloud, you have more than likely done so without *intent* behind it. **We do not intentionally screw up our day, week, month, or life; we do so unintentionally. And your life should be one of intent!**

So, an affirmation is first thought out _intentionally_, then written down and stated aloud – WITH INTENT – what you want from life as though you have already attained it. (You've probably noticed that intent plays a pretty important role here. Hence the all caps.)

What this means is that we do not simply want to state things like "I'm happy I'm happy I'm happy" with no emotion nor passion behind it. That's not affirming, that's just speaking aloud. Affirmations need to be stated with the intent to manifest each and every word into existence. [Let's run that back once more.] **Affirmations need to be stated with the intent to manifest each and every word into existence.**

When we are truly passionate/angry/sad about something, we speak with the intent of communicating and expressing the sentiment. Think about your last argument, debate over sports, or heated disagreement. Our hands move, we become animated, and the physical aspect of our being becomes just as important as the verbal. The same should be true for your affirmations when communicating them to yourself and the universe. In other words, you must *FEEL* what you are saying. Either believe it, or say it like you do, until you actually do. If you are not doing this, you will reap half-fulfilled results. It is true, that you get out what you put in.

It is completely acceptable and safe to get weird, privately or publicly, if you must. There are nights where I am alone, walking around my bed before going to sleep, physicalizing my words as I repeat my affirmations aloud, raising my voice and reaching my open palms upwards, then quickly snatching them down into balled up fist as I claim and take from the universe what is rightfully mine! Other nights my girlfriend is laying in bed watching me do this exact routine. You would undoubtedly pay good money to see the look on her face during this time.

There are moments before an interview, a performance, a public speaking event, or anything that requires my confidence to come out and play, where I will go find a mirror or quiet spot to repeat my affirmations aloud – completely willing to risk being caught whaling my arms around and talking to myself by a bystander in passing – and from time to time it happens! What I tell myself will forever be more important and vital to my success & well-being than what other people think. This truth is *non-negotiable*. Another important truth to know about affirmations, is that you can and should have multiple (for the various areas of your life), and **your affirmations can and will be constantly evolving as you grow**.

It is to my understanding that a lot of people don't know what the hell an affirmation even looks like, or where to start in regard to their own. If that is you, in the following pages I have placed a few affirmation templates for different areas of your life – to be adjusted, reworded, altered, and completely paraphrased by you, to better mold into valuable meaning in your life. If you already have your own, great! Maybe this serves as a kick-starter for some, and for others it may serve as fresh ideas to bounce off of. **Most importantly: there are no rules**. Your affirmations are YOURS, and YOURS alone. I would simply ask that you try to keep every word positive, and avoid heavy words like "not" or "don't". Speak as though whatever you want, is already yours! I promise I am not giving you rules, just asking! (For a more in-depth dive into affirmations for your day to day, check out *The Affirmation Booklet* – written by myself)

BEDTIME

Thank you for giving me these __ hours of sleep tonight. __ hours is exactly what I need to feel rested and _____ in the morning. My body is capable of miraculous things, the least of which is pulling together a big boost of energy from __ restful hours of sleep. I believe that I can create my experience of reality, and I choose to wake up tomorrow, feeling _____ and excited to take on my day, and I'm grateful for that.

WAKE UP

I am getting out of bed with purpose because I genuinely want to. I will continue to dedicate time each day to developing myself into the person I need to be to create the most _____, _____, and abundant life I can imagine. My wake up motivation level is on 10. I am thankful for the __ hours of sleep that I got, and my body is absolutely capable of functioning at high capacity for the entirety of my day.

MY DAY

I am a success. I am a _____. I am a _____. I am the greatest. I am the greatest version of myself right now in this moment. My internal dialogue, whether conscious or subconscious, is solely positive. Realistic, and still solely positive. I am not bound by my fears, insecurities, nor limitations of my past. My actions align with what

I want to accomplish, and who I need to be to accomplish them. I constantly transform the way I think and feel to overcome any and all limiting beliefs & behaviors and replace them with what's needed to succeed. I am in control of my destiny! I deserve to be _____! I am committed to doing everything I must do today to reach my goals and create the life of my dreams!

CONFIDENCE

I'm good enough, I'm smart enough, and to be completely honest with everyone in the room right now (even though it's just me), people love me! My inner voice tells me I'm _____, inspiring, _____, selfless, selfish when required, giving, outgoing, confident, _____, capable, adaptable, two steps ahead, maybe even 5 steps ahead, too strong, strong because I'm vulnerable, accessible, focused, _____, unstoppable, self-believing, and everything I need to be in order to become the person required to accomplish my biggest dreams. I will become that person. I am becoming that person. I am that person. I am THE person.

Before we head into our next topic, please remember that these are yours. Change them, customize them, whatever it takes. Just repeat these *consistently*. Eventually, you will know these by heart! You will hear your internal dialogue repeating them throughout your day, and your actions will follow. Your habits will change and begin to align with what you've now been telling yourself. Most importantly, your life will begin to reflect these words because your mind believes them to be true!

Your affirmations need to be strong enough to withstand the

resistance you will face in toxic environments. Some of us come from places, homes, relationships, and surroundings much more difficult to overcome than the typical person. If this is true for you, you may want to talk to yourself twice as much! In a toxic environment, negativity will present itself to you in more forms than you feel as though you can handle. You may hear negative affirmations toward you from the people closest to you – even family or spouses. This only increases the importance of you guarding yourself with an UNSHAKABLE mindset! When in a toxic environment…. MOVE! **If you're unable to move physically, change your MENTAL REAL ESTATE.** Move into a mental state of being where you can lock the gate from outsiders who are not breathing life into your vibe. Now that you know how, there is no excuse. One will give in – will it be your mindset or your environment?

THINK ABOUT YOUR LAST ARGUMENT, DEBATE OVER SPORTS, OR HEATED DISAGREEMENT. OUR HANDS MOVE, WE BECOME ANIMATED, AND THE PHYSICAL ASPECT OF OUR BEING BECOMES JUST AS IMPORTANT AS THE VERBAL. THE SAME SHOULD BE TRUE FOR YOUR AFFIRMATIONS WHEN COMMUNICATING THEM TO YOURSELF AND THE UNIVERSE.

5

How to face yourself

onesty with self. That's where this begins. You. Have. Got. To. Be. Honest. With. Yourself. Without this truth, you will most certainly live a half-fulfilled life. This is not an easy, nor practical feat. Facing yourself might actually require some impracticality; some breaking the norm. This is not a subject taught to us in school. It is more than likely not even a core value that your parents taught you growing up. Sure, they taught you not to lie, but that is not exercising the same muscle as being honest with yourself. Facing yourself might require that you break and, all on your lonesome, piece yourself together.

There's a saying that goes "you can only lead a horse to water, you cannot force it to drink." But why in the hell would the horse not want to drink the water it just followed you to? ... Maybe because that would require the horse to see its own reflection first.

The truth of the matter, and an unshakable fact is that everyone reading this right now wants to be a better version of themselves. Whether it be financially, physically, mentally, emotionally, spiritually, in our homes, at our craft, in our relationships, at our jobs, at our education, in our future, about our pasts, or just in general – we want to be better. Even the villains walking the planet want to be better at destroying things. But can we look at ourselves, see our flaws (or areas with room for improvement), and be accepting of them without judging ourselves?

The seemingly difficult part of becoming a version of ourselves that we currently are not, is that we must leave our current state of being, behind. This does not mean that literally everything about you must change, but **in regard to the next layer of yourself, the easiest way to *not* reach that is to remain exactly who you are right now. Just like the easiest way to *not* get where you want in life, is to stay exactly where you are right now.** More often than not, becoming better, stronger, smarter, faster, requires a push from within; and we tap out early in the process simply because it's safer and we don't have to change anything. This *tap out* almost always presents itself when we're at the point of breaking who we currently are. Watch out for this. Look out for it closely, until you are able to discern the difference between your body, mind, and spirit ACTUALLY needing to rest – or your subconscious trying make sure the current version of you lives on.

Here's something we often do in our lives… A good thing will present itself to us and we'll knowingly veer away from it, because it forces us to face ourselves, maybe even makes us better, but most importantly does not allow us to remain who we are. A habit will have to change, a routine will get disrupted, an insecurity will get exposed, something will have to be sacrificed, or something might break. [Hopefully I haven't lost you, but if I have, allow me to break this down further.]

The reason why you have multiple alarms in the morning is not because you love being woken up over and over again. It is because *you know* waking up at 5am requires you to say 'no' to the version of you that currently snoozes until 7am. It's easier to sleep in; we fall in love with the idea of more sleep (or remaining where we are), and so we do. Some of us are not yet at the point of honesty with self to face that. It is more comfortable, familiar, and easy to *not* change our behavioral patterns and choices; so we'll give ourselves some sort of excuse to justify why we have multiple alarms instead. We'll give ourselves an excuse as to why we should not try to push through that last rep at the gym. We'll give ourselves an excuse as to why we cannot love wholeheartedly. We'll give ourselves an EXCUSE as to why we are unable to change our diet, or unable to go skydiving, or don't have time to read, or why we're stuck, etc. Again – **we cannot be who we are and who we want to be at the same time. One has to give. Which one are you giving in to?**

By nature, our brains are designed to help us survive. Survival is the best friend of safety; and feeling safe is a byproduct of familiarity. So by putting this together, we can easily see and understand that our brains love what is familiar to them. In order to keep us safe (aka who we are right now), our brains will feed us lines, thoughts, and reasons as to why we should remain in this *familiar* territory. **THE CURRENT YOU KNOWS THAT IT WILL BE BROKEN AND LEFT BEHIND IN THE PROCESS OF YOU BECOMING YOUR NEXT BEST SELF. This is precisely why we turn to old habits that we KNOW hold us back.**

The whole point of practicing honesty with ourselves is to get to the point where we can distinguish between what our brains are feeding us out of fear... and the unfiltered truth as to what we actually need.

And so... We've come all this way in this chapter to get to this point. The **HOW**. How do you face yourself? In order to make this practical, and something that you can easily apply, let's call upon one of the practices that all great leaders indulge in: **taking responsibility for everything that goes wrong, and giving credit for everything that goes right.** This is EXTREMELY IMPORTANT, and one of the key practices to put into place in order to face yourself, better yourself, and change your life for the better. [I'll explain, keep reading.]

Really think about this for a second. If we blame someone or some thing for what's happening or has happened in our lives, we essentially have just given that person or thing full power over the direction of our lives. I'm imploring you not to argue this one. This is a fact. The second that you acknowledge a person, place, thing, situation, or circumstance as the determining factor of an outcome in YOUR life, you SUBMIT your throne as Queen/King of YOUR WORLD.

A friend of mine, named Sickamore (who doesn't know me – I'll explain later in *How to change your group of friends*) once said "Master yourself, and you will master your world." I'm here to tell you that facing yourself is a direct channel to mastering yourself. **In order to face yourself, you MUST identify and accept the YOU in all areas of your life. Blaming and pointing your finger at anything or anyone besides the person in your selfie lens relieves you of your duty to better yourself**. And because this is so easy and requires no work whatsoever, 99% of the earth's population is doing it. It's not cool anymore – let yourself know, then go tell a friend. Then come back and take a second to **embrace the responsibility to shift the aspects of your life that are not yet where you want them to be.**

Something special lies on the other side of this change – the better, more enlightened, more creative, more capable, more powerful, and more aware version of you. Here's why – now that you've accepted the challenge and responsibility of molding yourself and your world, your focus suddenly moves from what's going on **around** you to what's going on *within* you. This is called taking charge of your life. The process of claiming the power you have been blessed with allows you to first SEE it. If you are looking elsewhere to find understanding or the source of things not going the way that you want, you've already lost. **You've lost because accountability has no peripheral**. It does not involve looking externally. It is the continuous choice and conscious effort to ask yourself "**what can I do better?**" – even when there is seemingly nothing that you could have done better. It's not actually about the question; it's the truth of the mindset behind the question. That truth is the following: no one, no thing, no place, no situation, nor circumstance is in control of your life. And on the flip side of that is also this truth: no one, no thing, no place, no situation, nor circumstance is capable of having an impact on your life greater than your own.

This does take sacrifice. I mean REAL sacrifice. Like the kind of sacrifice required to be right, but not say it aloud in order to feed your ego. An ego doesn't need feeding. Starve it, and from doing so, an even greater version of yourself will grow. Take responsibility for dealing with everything that goes wrong - THIS is how you face yourself. Be greater. "Master yourself, and you will master your world."

ACCOUNTABILITY HAS NO PERIPHERAL. IT DOES NOT INVOLVE LOOKING EXTERNALLY. IT IS THE CONTINUOUS CHOICE AND CONSCIOUS EFFORT TO ASK YOURSELF "WHAT CAN I DO BETTER?" – EVEN WHEN THERE IS SEEMINGLY NOTHING THAT YOU COULD HAVE DONE BETTER. IT'S NOT ACTUALLY ABOUT THE QUESTION; IT'S THE TRUTH OF THE MINDSET BEHIND THE QUESTION.

6

The Word "Can't" Should Not Be In Your Vocabulary

This one is really close to the heart for me. I could not be more passionate in the belief that there is absolutely NO valuable use for this word in the human vocabulary. I do not believe in inability. I believe in us. I believe in our ability to figure out what is required in order to DO. The fact that knowledge of this word is being passed down from generation to generation in itself is heart-wrenching. Children especially, do not need to know this word. There's no need for it! And I'm very confident in our ability to continue onward in life without it. [That concludes my rant and now we'll get into why this was deemed important enough to be deserving of its own chapter.]

If you've read the *Do You Even Affirmation Bro? Sis?* or *Brainwash Yourself 101* chapters, then you now understand the power of words and the intent that they signal to our brains, which then have a direct impact on our actions, which in turn has an impact on the outcome of our lives. To avoid delaying where we're going with this, lets just outright say it now: **the minute that we say something "can't" be done, our brains shut down.** Particularly, they shut down the neurological pathways that would have otherwise lead us down the road to HOW something seemingly impossible could actually be done. Why on earth (or any planet for that matter) would we want to limit our capabilities? It amazes me how much of **what we believe to possible relies on what we communicate to ourselves.** Um, in case you have not picked up on what's being said here... **WHAT WE COMMUNICATE TO OURSELVES CAN ACTUALLY CHANGE OUR REALM OF POSSIBILITIES.**

By saying we "can't" do something, we're admitting to, submitting to, and accepting defeat before even giving ourselves a chance. This immediately CREATES another barrier in our lives that doesn't need to be there. Picture a bird, very much capable of flying, reluctantly *walking* into a cage, before even flapping it's wings – that's the equivalent to using the word "can't". Think of this metaphor every time you hear the word.

This book is not just about the behaviors we must do in order to create the life we want, it's also about the behaviors we must STOP doing. Everyone knows how difficult it is to create and enforce new habits in our lives, but for this chapter lets look at how detrimental it can be when we don't let go of old ones. I can almost guarantee that the word "can't" does not align with where you want to go in life and who you want to be. And I'm using the word here as a tangible vessel for you to see, but what we're really talking about is the thought process behind this word, and how limiting it can be.

We are gathered here to be empowered and unlock the unstoppable-ness within ourselves. In order to solidify this ideology, lets bring in some science-backed research...

So, a couple of researchers at Boston College and University of Houston made some very interesting discoveries around the power of words – particularly in this study, the words "don't" and "can't". They can seem very similar when placed into statements like: "I *don't* eat bread" or "I *can't* eat bread". In all actuality, **they are very different** –

at least how your brain translates each.

Heidi Grant Halvorson Ph. D., in an article on *Psychology Today*, states "***I don't*** is experienced as a **choice**, so it feels empowering. It's an affirmation of your determination and will power. ***I can't*** isn't a choice; it's a **restriction**, it's being imposed upon you. Thinking 'I can't' undermines your sense of power and personal agency." [Wow]

If we're being completely honest with ourselves, everything we do, say, and think is a choice – true power lies in the realization and acceptance of this. It's time we stop giving our power away, especially to words like "can't".

Why are we placing such emphasis and focus on something so small as eliminating the word "can't" from our vocabulary? As if changing this one thing is going magically poof everything we want into existence? Because it will! Of course not right away, but it's THE start. **Eliminating this word requires consciously practicing the choice to not say it when the opportunity presents itself** *– and that is actively forcing it out of your life.*

THIS BOOK IS NOT JUST ABOUT THE BEHAVIORS WE MUST DO IN ORDER TO CREATE THE LIFE WE WANT, IT'S ALSO ABOUT THE BEHAVIORS WE MUST STOP DOING.

7

It Doesn't Get Better In Time. You Do.

As we move forward in all things revolving around bettering ourselves, some old skin is going to be shed. Sayings like "it will be okay" or "it'll all get better in time" come from a good place, and often are simply words meant to comfort us. Although they may seem harmless, when we remove the fluff, the truth of the matter is they are not *empowering*. They don't scream I AM CAPABLE. Sayings like these imply that if we just sit it out and wait, magic will occur and one day we'll live happily ever after. Um, no.

Throughout this book, a consistent theme has been navigating through life with a special care and attentiveness to the words we become reliant on – it applies here as well. Too often we see people energetically and mentally paralyze themselves, and what's actually needed is an improvement within. Change is not as much a byproduct of time, as it is a byproduct of action. *Change is not as much a byproduct of time, as it is a byproduct of action.* CHANGE IS NOT AS MUCH A BYPRODUCT OF TIME, AS IT IS A BYPRODUCT OF ACTION.

The reason we often repeat our undesirable experiences is because it's extremely easy to. All we have to do is the same exact thing we've been doing: tell ourselves it'll get better, and that change is coming, but then do/think/speak nothing different. This state of being is very passenger-seaty. Things are happening to and around you, you don't like it, and yet you're convinced that it will get better. No one is judging here…but THIS IS LAZY. It's inactive. It's repetitive. It's unattractive and counterproductive to the human spirit, and extremely addictive to the human brain because not too much has to be done on top of the 3,000 other thoughts you're dealing with every hour. The lovely and promising reality is that WE still have a choice to get better in time. Better yet, now that you're reading this book, YOU have a *responsibility* to get better in time.

What a beautiful word. *Responsibility*. The ability to respond. Ah. Yes. It's not so heavy when you look at it that way. It's not some chore that you absolutely have to do. Truthfully, if you would like, you can do nothing at all. **But just be aware that you do have the ABILITY to do** more – that is what we're tapping into here. This slight shift in how we look at life and what we expect from it, IS the difference between someone waiting for life to get better and someone like you who is actively taking steps to live a better life.

So how to we make this practical? How do we apply it in real time when life has the wind blowing into our faces? The answer is ***intent***. [Stick with me for a second here and let me explain.] **Ask yourself what you *intend* to do, think, and speak**. That's a super general question but have you genuinely asked and answered that for yourself? What's uniquely powerful about this question is that it acknowledges the truth that uncontrollable things will occur, AND at the same time, reinforces the bigger truth, which is that YOU HAVE THE ABILITY TO PRE-DETERMINE HOW YOU COME OUT ON THE OTHER SIDE OF ANYTHING THAT BREAKS YOU, IMPEDES YOUR PROCESS, OR PUNCHES YOU IN THE FACE.

When you set an intent for what you want out of life, you place yourself in a position to '***show up different***' to almost anything.

Showing up different **means rearranging, shifting, elevating, and positioning whatever necessary in your core-being to approach anything in life... but in a state that is greater than the version of you that was once susceptible to the downside of certain things**. This is important because issues in your life are not going to alter their degree of difficulty. *Alcohol is alcohol with or without an alcoholic attached to it - it's how a person shows up to alcohol that determines its effect. Bills will remain bills with or without you and your income. Your past is your past whether you like it or not. Your boss is terrible whether you're working for them or not. The weather is going to do what it will tomorrow, no matter how you feel about it. If earth wants to quake, it's going to quake.* **CIRCUMSTANCE DOES NOT CARE ABOUT HOW YOU FEEL, WHAT YOU DO OR DON'T DO, NOR WHAT YOU SAY ABOUT IT**. So saying "it'll get better in time" is a joke. *EITHER YOU WILL 'SHOW UP DIFFERENT' TO YOUR CHALLENGES OR NOT. EITHER YOU WILL GET BETTER IN TIME OR NOT.* Trust me, the circumstance does not change. YOU change, and life reflects that. Or you don't, and the challenges seemingly get worse and worse – even though it's *you* who's getting worse – BECAUSE IF YOU'RE NOT GETTING BETTER, YOU'RE GETTING... [*you name it*].

Your completion of this chapter solidifies your intent to speak, think, and do things that manifest whatever you desire from life. Say it aloud so that your subconscious can hear it too: I INTEND TO SPEAK, THINK, AND DO THINGS THAT MANIFEST WHATEVER I DESIRE FROM LIFE.

Consciously choosing to be **intentional** about LIVING OUT what you're capable of - that's being truly empowered. It's either that, or disempowering yourself and leaving it up to "things" getting better. Nah. You get better. *Intend* to show up different.

CIRCUMSTANCE DOES NOT CARE ABOUT HOW YOU FEEL, WHAT YOU DO OR DON'T DO, NOR WHAT YOU SAY ABOUT IT. SO SAYING "IT'LL GET BETTER IN TIME" IS A JOKE. EITHER YOU WILL 'SHOW UP DIFFERENT' TO YOUR CHALLENGES OR NOT. EITHER YOU WILL GET BETTER IN TIME OR NOT.

8

How to Face Your Fears

The popular suggestion around facing fears is leaning into them, and it usually rides behind the sentiment of sayings such as - "Just do it." Although there is plenty truth to the fact that, at the end of the day, you have to execute and take action…the "how" has been greatly overlooked time and time again. Let's peel a few layers back and acknowledge that *our fears are simply an extension of ourselves* - thus yet again, bringing things back to YOU. How fun, right? Well, yes, this is where it can get extremely fun.

Your fears are a reflection of your being, your self-made limitations, your experiences, your perspective, the limitations that were made FOR you, and ultimately where your greatest unfamiliarity lie. The straight-shot to facing fears may be just jumping in, but here's an alternative: **learn about them.** When you learn, you expand your familiarity, and in turn, shrink the size of your fear. The greater your unfamiliarity, the greater your fear. **The greater your familiarity, the greater your courage**. The quickest path to familiarity is personal experience, the 2nd quickest path is someone else's.

Be weary of your fear being so great that you allow it to affect your willingness to listen and learn from someone else's experience of whatever it is that you're afraid of. If you fear skydiving, and are not yet at the point to experience it personally, learn from/talk to/research someone who has and BE CURIOUS. **IF THERE BE ANYTHING THAT YOU FEAR, AND HAVE NOT DECIDED TO EXPERI-ENCE IT PERSONALLY, SEEK OUT PEOPLE WHO HAVE AND BE CURIOUS.** The cool thing about applying this is two-fold: on one end you'll end up expanding your knowledge of something, and on the other end, you'll end up shrinking your fear of it. You can do this without actually "doing it". There is no real alibi for a lack of curiosity however; especially when it pertains to something you fear.

Take your eyes off of whatever it is that you fear, look inward, and realize that the feeling of fear is a signal from within yourself screaming that **you can expand who you are**. That is what you are ultimately facing - you. By investing in yourself for the purpose of expanding who you are, you will grow your knowledge of many things that you may not currently understand. Fear is fed by remaining stagnant; courage is fed by curiosity, knowledge, and experience. Here's the secret sauce: **you can either live in fear, and avoid facing your lack of self-expansion, or you grow to the point that you show up differently to things that you once feared**. The things we fear typically don't change or go away. Fear doesn't actually go away at all; what happens is an internal expansion of self...to the point of overriding & suffocating what are usually false, limiting beliefs. I encourage you to go expand - be it through your own experiences, or from the second-hand smoke of someone else's. Just don't go through life fearing something you never invested the time to fully understand.

HERE'S THE SECRET SAUCE: YOU CAN EITHER LIVE IN FEAR, AND AVOID FACING YOUR LACK OF SELF-EXPANSION, OR YOU GROW TO THE POINT THAT YOU SHOW UP DIFFERENTLY TO THINGS THAT YOU ONCE FEARED.

9

How To Change Your Group Of Friends

O k...ok. We've all heard the saying – "you become like the 5 people you hang around most" – or some variation of those words. [Maybe "you are an average of the 5 people you spend the most time with".] Either way, I've got a bone to pick with whoever made up this saying, or maybe my beef is just with the quote itself. Yes, there's tons of truth to it. But it fails to address an even greater truth: that being that IN REAL LIFE YOU DON'T JUST DROP YOUR FRIENDS AND MOVE ONTO THE NEXT GROUP. We normal people have this thing called loyalty. Code of ethics. Etc. Just because our friends aren't as lit as we are in regard to personal development (or insert whatever it is you're after), does not mean we're okay with ditching the empire of inside jokes we have built up over the years, to go radically changing the average of people around us. Also....if I want to be a millionaire, but I'm not one yet (and none of my friends are), chances are other millionaires aren't the most accessible to me, nor have any desire to hang out with me. I'd bring down their average! (If we're being petty and technical about the quote)

I'll contradict myself and what I just said at the end of the previous paragraph in a bit here, but let's proceed as we normally would for now. This is for the folk out there who are pursuing something that their 5 closest people are not. The folk who want to be millionaires and beyond, but personally know none. The folk who WANT to up their game, but don't currently have someone in their immediate circle who is operating at a higher vibration (no shade to our current friends). Here is how to beat the system...

CONSUME MORE OF THE STUFF THAT LIFTS YOU UP, FROM THE PEOPLE THAT FIRE YOU UP. [I could be childish and end the chapter here, but I actually want to be liked by you, so I'll explain.] In your quest to become the Yoda of your field (aka master of your world), you will more than likely reach a point where the people around you are unable to match your drive, intensity, passion, willingness to learn, etc. It is at this point, where you will need to change your group of friends, without completely parting ways from the friendships you have built. YOU CAN DO BOTH.

Fortunately for us, this day and age provides us with access to the greatest people walking the planet. And fortunately for you, I have studied how to study these greats and become friends with them. **We are what we eat. That can also be translated to we are what we consume. This essentially means that we become more of what we consume the most**. And THAT means, if you want to increase your 'average' (of being), then you need to consume higher level material. Allow me to break this down...

Let's say that you want to want to be more positive. Cool, very admirable. Only thing is, no one around you is – everyone you know is complaining and talking about the next person (no judgement, it happens). Your *responsibility* now is to find more positive material. This could be a TV show, a podcast, a book, a radio show, a movie, a dog, a dope view in your neighborhood, solitary confinement, whatever. Whatever it is, go consume more of it. And more. And even more on top of that. Create a collection of go-to positive material to dive into, and then STAY in it, or engulf yourself in it as frequently as possible. As a result, what WILL happen, is you WILL become more positive. But be more consistent with this than you do anything else in your life. At the least, be as consistent with practicing this as you are with hanging out with friends.

This same rule applies if you're the only one in your group who wants to ride motorcycles, write a book, start a business, move out of your hometown, change your diet, launch the next google, fly to space, meditate until you elevate, play professional sports, or pet dogs. Whatever it is that you want to do, find people that already do it (or something close to it), and consume everything they are sharing until you can recite it better than they can. You are NOT an average of the 5 people you spend the most time with. YOU ARE AN AVERAGE OF WHAT YOU CONSUME THE MOST. [One more time, louder for the people in the back? Sure.] You are NOT an average of the 5 people you spend the most time with. YOU ARE AN AVERAGE OF WHAT YOU CONSUME THE MOST. Whether that's 5 friends, 5 uplifting podcasts, 5 hours on TikTok, or 5 cheeseburgers in a day - you'll become an average of what you're consuming. Don't be a cheeseburger.

Rather than focusing on changing *just* your group of friends, start by focusing on what you consume. What music are you listening to? What TV shows are you watching? Where are you hanging out? What are you eating? How are these things helping you create the life you want? How are these things putting more money into your bank account? How are these things contributing to your happiness and well-being? How long does the "high" last from these things?

Whatever it is that you want to do or be, lean into consuming stuff from people who have done, are doing, or *are* it. And when you find those people, STAY AROUND WHATEVER THEY ARE SHARING. Hang out with their material for hours, the same way you hang out with your friends for hours. Binge listen to their

podcasts, binge watch their Instagram videos, binge read their books, binge attend their events! Keep doing it until you are brainwashed by their greatness, and continue to cultivate your own.

The rules have changed. You now get to filter what comes into your world. What's amazing is how people will *want* to become wealthy, but consume poor material. Don't be that person. If you want to own a house, consume something about owning a house from someone who's done it or more. If you want to move out of your town or city, consume information from someone who HAS or more. If you are listening to broke people talk about how to get rich, then you are most likely consuming the wrong material. If you want to change your life, keeping up with the Kardashians, or the next episode of 'Power' probably won't cut it! **You can still watch shows and do things for enjoyment, but make sure you also consume things that are going to help push you forward, ignite you, inform you, inspire you, and give you actionable steps on what to do in order to get you where you want to be.**

The universe is now, more than ever, a GPS to the life of your dreams. Yet you're typing "where are we going for happy hour this Friday" in your search box. Or "When does Game of Thrones drop next?" Or "Who am I dating next?" Or simply not typing anything in your search box at all! That ends here. You are way too capable of more. If you don't want more for yourself, more for the people around you, more for the world, or more out of life in general – you do not have to continue reading this book. This book is for the folk who for some reason, feel something greater within themselves, or want to discover the most this life has to offer them.

My best friends are Will Smith, Mother Theresa, Hal Elrod, Grant Cardone, Chaka Bars, Oprah Winphrey, Steve Jobs, Ghandi, MLK Jr., Bill Gates, Arnold Schwarzeneggar, Ellen Degeneres, Vishen Lakhiani,

Jay Shetty, Michael Phelps, Kobe Bryant, Terry Cruz, 14th Dalai Lama, Gary Vee, Alex Honnold, Jay Z, and so many more. The most intriguing thing is...none of them know me. I just consume almost everything they share for 99% of my day. So if you were wondering...yes, my mind is lit... and at all times - thanks to my friends.

You can find the people you need in your life long before you are ACTUALLY friends with them. Consume what they share about their journey, and as a result, your journey will lead you to the real-life people you need to meet.

YOU CAN FIND THE PEOPLE YOU NEED IN YOUR LIFE LONG BEFORE YOU ARE ACTUALLY FRIENDS WITH THEM. CONSUME WHAT THEY SHARE ABOUT THEIR JOURNEY, AND AS A RESULT, YOUR JOURNEY WILL LEAD YOU TO THE REAL-LIFE PEOPLE YOU NEED TO MEET.

10

Balance is BS. Seek Harmony.

Aggressive title, I know – but we've got to speak on it. It's gone way too far, and I'm sick of seeing people settle – that also stops here. For far too long, the term "balance" has implicitly suggested that areas of our lives are separate entities that need to be juggled – this is just not the case. The undeniable truth of the matter is…every single part of our lives is connected in some way, shape, or form. Usually the connecting piece is YOU.

What I mean by "connected" in this particular context is that the various areas of our lives are holistically inseparable. Your physical being is connected to your emotional being which is connected to your spiritual being which is connected to your mental being, the same way your work life is connected to your relationship life which is connected to your social life which is connected to your financial life which is connected to your dream life which is connected to your goals and aspirations which is connected to your family life which is connected to your business life which is…okay, you see where I'm going with this. When I hear someone imply that trying to balance these areas is best, I question how plausible that is. Our lives are far too complex to try to balance all these areas. That word 'balance', at least to this guy, has evidently placed us as a human race in positions where certain areas of our lives get left behind due to neglect. While we're trying to balance one area, we turn our back on the others, and by the time we get back to the others, the one area we got to balance is now unbalanced again.

Let's take the famous term "work-life balance" for example. It makes me sick to my stomach just writing it. It's old and dated – sorry, not sorry. I am actually making the argument that we can do better, based on the fact that I have seen far more people lose control of their *life* (and/or areas of it) while executing and excelling in their *career* (and vice versa), than people who have excelled in their career and also improved their quality of life simultaneously. The few who have and are excelling in multiple areas at the same time are not balancing – they are harmonizing. Let me explain...

One thing we'll probably never see is a maestro (aka band conductor) completely turn his or her back on the drum section in order to signal the string section to play. No matter what's going on during a performance, be it a solo or crescendo (gradual increase in loudness [for my non-musical experts]) from a particular section, the maestro faces the entire band – with the goal being one united sound, better known as harmony. A complete orchestra is made up of so many moving parts: flutes, trumpets, saxophones, drums, violins, bass, strings, and more! One of the most beautiful things about a performance is that no one section is more important than the other – each contributes equally to the movement of sound – and so it is with life. We have careers, relationships, friendships, family, time, physical health, emotional health, spiritual health, diets, leisure, finances, and more! **You are the maestro of your life, and no one area is more important than the other**. (We may prioritize one over another, but that does not make one less important than another)

"Work-life balance" typically suggests that we should work our jobs, and then take care of our lives outside of those work hours; or lets just call it what it is - focus on your dreams, goals, and everything else outside of those work hours. I am not saying that this is wrong or can't be done this way. I'm saying that it's outdated, and no longer the most efficient or viable way of going about things. *What if your job was in harmony with your dreams? What if your relationship/partner was in harmony with your passion and career goals? What if your friendships and social life were in harmony with your time (that there's never enough of)? What if your passion was in harmony with your purpose?*

We all know people (maybe even yourself) who are currently working or have worked a job that pays the bills, and then using the rest of the hours of the day to do the things that they REALLY want to do. Not only is physical energy being exerted into the "job", but so is emotional, creative, mental, and spiritual energy as well. Which means the things that we REALLY want to be doing are not even getting our best energy or our most effective time of day. This also means the things and people that 100% deserve our best energy and effectiveness are not either.

The orchestra/band and 'work-life' are just examples. Lock in on the message behind the examples, which is that when we attempt to balance the various areas of our lives, we more than often fall short in some areas because our focus is everywhere except for where it is needed the most… you've probably guessed it by now – on ourselves. Stick with me here.

I'm literally shaking as I'm writing this because I can feel you getting closer to understanding your full potential and how to tap into it. Ultimately, what we want is for each area of our lives to flourish. **We work extremely hard on these things [careers, relationships, finances, etc] and that's great but these very things can become a distraction and an illusion that we end up chasing while completely leaving ourselves behind – and this is the reason for the misalignment and lack of harmony. That thing you are chasing, that feeling, that moment, that light-bulb, that**

BALANCE IS BS. SEEK HARMONY.

burning desire, and the very reason you are reading this book right now is NOT something external. It is YOU. Give yourself permission right now to stop chasing *betterment of the areas* of your life. That's a given [that we want that]! Give yourself permission right now to chase ***betterment of you***! From the inside! Give yourself 100% permission to do this because the truth of the matter is **we do not have to balance these things in order to achieve our most fulfilling life. All we must do is harmonize from the inside out. When we do this, the law of attraction can actually come out and play! All the areas of your life, the people in your life, and what you want out of life will become magnets to the entirety of your being. And rather than reaching out externally to juggle and balance everything, the areas of your life will find the rhythm and harmony on their own BECAUSE of YOUR direction,** you incredibly dope maestro. It's also important to note that the members of your 'band' who are playing out of key and shouldn't be there...will reveal themselves to you, so that you may be able to respectfully and lovingly remove them from your stage and maybe even out of your life.

Let me translate that for those who lost me during the analogy: **when you focus on aligning yourself BEFORE everything else in your life, the areas of your life where you desire success and fulfillment will naturally level up as a byproduct of you harmonizing within first. In that very same regard, by being in alignment with yourself *first*, anything or anyone who is not in alignment with who you are, who you are becoming, where you are going, and what you are trying to build...will become easily recognizable and identifiable to you – allowing you to see clearly enough who or what you need to respectfully and lovingly remove from your life.**

The reason for this bias against balance lies in the fact that it places awareness to the many things on the scale – but not the actual scale itself. If the scale (you) is broken, nothing's getting balanced anyway. When your focus is divided on the various areas of your life, that much less of it is on yourself – which leads to unevenness and a lack of balance. Harmony requires a much more whole version of you; and **a WHOLE YOU is the goal because that is PRECISELY what you would feel if all the areas of your life were aligned and where you wanted them to be**. Stop chasing the things on the scale, and make the scale a magnet. Every area of your life is an extension of you.

Balance: a situation in which different elements are equal or in the correct proportions.

Photo Credit: https://www.123rf.com

Harmony: the quality of forming a pleasing or consistent whole.

Photo Credit: https://www.123rf.com

WHEN YOU FOCUS ON ALIGNING YOURSELF BEFORE EVERYTHING ELSE IN YOUR LIFE, THE AREAS OF YOUR LIFE WHERE YOU DESIRE SUCCESS AND FULFILLMENT WILL NATURALLY LEVEL UP AS A BYPRODUCT OF YOU HARMONIZING WITHIN FIRST.

11

Active Force or Die

O ne of the most valuable things you can take away from this book is the understanding that IF THERE IS NO ACTIVE FORCE AGAINST WHAT WOULD NATURALLY OCCUR, THEN THE NATURAL WILL OCCUR. By this point in our lives, most things are a part of our human nature as a result of what we were taught. Some of these things are good, and others are things like the word 'can't'. In order to reverse, eliminate, or compensate for negative processes in our lives, we must be extra INTENTIONAL about the positive ones. If we do nothing, what has happened will simply continue to happen.

What the hell is an active force? I'm glad you asked. In this book, and in your life, **it's something that you consciously have in place, or are doing, saying, or thinking in order to produce a desired outcome.** How do you know it's active? Well, **your desired outcome would more than likely not happen if you did not have this active force in place.**

*[In physiology, interestingly enough, **active force** is calculated by subtracting passive force from total force. Basically this means (in our translation) that life will happen (total force), by nature and whether or not*

you do anything (passive force), and what you are doing (active force) is what is left.]

This truth reveals itself in so many ways where we can apply an active force. Take for example, financial wealth. Most people are unable to achieve the financial success they desire because there are not enough *active forces* against their natural expenses (such as living expenses). Someone can genuinely desire wealth but spend the entirety of their life without any because their only active force against their spending is their job income. If you want to make a million dollars, it may help to consume some sort of content that teaches you how - that would be an example of *actively* doing something in order to produce a desired outcome.

Lots of friendships, relationships, and marriages fail or fall short of their full potential due to lack of ACTIVE FORCES to keep them blossoming. Too frequently, people assume that things will just get better, with time (which we discussed in chapter 7), or just by nature. This could not be farther from the truth. Actively seeking ways to reach new depths and heights to our friendships, relationships, and marriages are how we not only make them last, but also grow! Trust me, just being in a relationship with someone will not make it last. (We'll talk more about that in the chapter titled **How To Make Your Relationship Last Forever**) The same is true for our friendships and marriages.

The last example we'll use here is life itself. This thing will 100% slap you around, fall apart, bypass you, leave you behind, punch you in the face, not say sorry afterwards, completely disrupt every plan you've ever had, and take away everything and maybe even everyone you've ever loved…UNLESS you create an active force in favor of the experience of life that you want. And yes, the truth is even when we do this, nothing is guaranteed. But we're currently learning to embrace and chase OURSELVES rather than results and outcomes, right? That is why we're all here right now. Anything guaranteed to us in this lifetime, any results, will be a byproduct of the most important active force that can exist – YOU.

Choosing not to level up within will result in what will naturally occur; and that is most likely not the life nor outcome that you want. **Life does not just get better on its own. Action must be taken, and on a day to day basis. Every single millisecond of our day is, in FACT, an opportunity to actively force the next millisecond to bend in our favor.** Will you be passive? Or Active? Be actively [insert whatever you want out of life], not just because everyone's doing it or saying it, but because if you don't, the universe, the world, and life itself, by nature won't be inclined to just hand it to you.

LIFE DOES NOT JUST GET BETTER ON ITS OWN. ACTION MUST BE TAKEN, AND ON A DAY TO DAY BASIS. EVERY SINGLE MILLISECOND OF OUR DAY IS, IN FACT, AN OPPORTUNITY TO ACTIVELY FORCE THE NEXT MILLISECOND TO BEND IN OUR FAVOR.

12

Get Off Tinder and Bumble. Don't Look For Your Soulmate. That's Not How Souls Mate.

To those who feel attacked by the title of this chapter: don't. We're not here to be called out on what we're doing right or wrong [see chapter titled *There Is No Right Or Wrong Way*]; we're here to discuss how we can be better and create better lives for ourselves. Let's get straight to it.

Allow me to start by stating a fact: there are an abundant amount of beautiful, healthy relationships that were birthed on dating sites, and it still happens to this day. But how did this whole meeting/matching people online thing even begin? What is arguably the first dating site created, started due to an engineer at Stanford going through a breakup with his girlfriend at the time. Shortly after, he took a hard look around and realized that he spent majority of his time in a classroom full of men. He states, "The odds were bad and I had to look elsewhere." (*credit: Nadja Sayej via VICE*)

It is very much understood that some people live a certain type of life, have a particular schedule, or personality that does not exactly make dating easy; nor does it allow for your soulmate to easily fall into your lap. For some, a dating site or app may seemingly be the best option. I have a few hiccups around this however, one being that, for a lot of people, the reasons above are not why they are on dating sites. So let's just get brutally honest here…you, or someone you know does the whole dating site/app thing for the following reasons: loneliness, boredom, distraction, it's Friday night, sex, looking for love, looking for connection, confidence (or the lack thereof), variety, attention, belief that no one in close proximity is worth looking at, validation from others, or just checking to see if we've "still got it". **Each of these reasons (in some way, shape, or form) fall under looking for love or connection**. Again, this is not about whether these reasons are right or wrong. The more important topic to address is how these reasons serve us. Are these reasons setting us up for what we want or what we need? Is what we want or need what's best for us?

Look, you may or may not have missed the part where I stated that all of the above reasons somehow fall under looking for love/connection – whether it be intentionally or unintentionally, consciously or subconsciously, there is an intent when we login to these sites/apps. Identifying that intent (and tending to the core of it), or choosing not to, can be the difference between a better you, and you swiping unwanted toxicity into your life. An uneasy truth is that most people have not tended to the core of their intent, more importantly, have not even tended to themselves. This is why we are all witness to the fact that an overwhelming amount of people on dating sites/apps are in many ways unhealed – and evidence of that sometimes presents itself before we even meet with the person on the other side of the screen!

Although dating sites/apps may have been conceptualized from a good place, what has happened over the years is they have attracted and become nesting grounds for people who are searching externally for things they have not yet found or tended to within. It's not that we become monsters once we sign up for Tinder, Bumble, Match.com, etc. It's more so that two lonely people does not necessarily equal a fulfilled connection – it more than likely just equals two lonely people. Two distracted people does not necessarily equal a focused connection – that more than likely just equals two people using one another for distraction. Two people looking for love does not necessarily equal a love connection, and two people looking for a connection does not necessarily mean they will connect. Imagine two separate people who are lost, walking through a forest, coming to find one another - this doesn't mean they've found what they're looking for - it just means we now have two lost people together. Also, two people looking for just sex rarely happens (it's usually one of the two people), and even when it does, they are either doing something or not doing something in their lives that has led them to the point where they have to look for it – rather than attract it – and that can be dangerous. **What is for certain is that the time being spent looking for something in someone else, can be more effectively spent adding value to yourself and looking for love & connection within**. I would go as far to say that **until we find love and connection within ourselves for ourselves, we won't even be able to fully receive that from someone else**.

This comes down to really creating the time to identify the feeling you have in the moment your fingers move to open one of these sites/apps. It comes down to being honest with ourselves and admitting that we are more than likely doing this to fill a gap or empty space within ourselves. How effective can it be to seek out fulfillment needed within, from someone you've never met, who is more than likely seeking the same thing? Two empty people does not equal filling each other's cups. YOU must be FULL in order to even have something substantial to pour in someone else's cup, and vice versa. That empty feeling we have after sleeping with someone is called connection without fulfillment.

Love and connection in their purest forms first happen within oneself, which carries with it fulfillment. The dating sites/apps are not the issue here – it is the act of seeking love/connection without finding that within first, and believing that someone else can fulfill what you're truly desiring and longing after. **We can, and more than likely will find temporary satisfaction over and over and over again through different people. That's easy. But filling your cup is not the same as fulfilling your cup. We will remain empty until we fulfill from the inside. Temporary satisfaction on repeat is not living (at least not at your full potential), and it sure does not equal fulfillment.**

A brilliant man by the name of Tony Robbins once said that we as humans ultimately have 6 needs: certainty, variety, significance, connection & love, growth, and to contribute beyond ourselves. Which one are you after when you login to a dating site/app? At what expense, or who's expense, are you willing to find it?

The core of each of the needs mentioned above can be found right within the doors of who you are – I say this in particular, from experience and what I have learned from some of the most fulfilled people walking the planet. I have personally spent years dancing around these 6 needs in a few ways. The first was not seeking these needs at all, and just existing. The second was seeking these needs from other people and things. The third was finally seeking these needs from within myself. Not only have I found them, but I also continue to, because I am infinite. **We are infinite**. That is precisely why I am adamantly writing for you in this book the following: within you, lies an infinite amount of certainty, variety, significance, connection & love, growth, and ability to contribute beyond yourself.

[*WITHIN YOU, LIES AN INFINITE AMOUNT OF CERTAINTY, VARIETY, SIGNIFICANCE, CONNECTION & LOVE, GROWTH, AND ABILITY TO CONTRIBUTE BEYOND YOURSELF.*]

It is during your journey of using every ounce of your literal, physical, spiritual, emotional, imaginative, energetic, and even incomprehensible power to find these needs within yourself...that you will have a very high likelihood of meeting your soulmate (or whatever other term you call this person), and they will more than likely be on that very same journey within themselves. What's arguably even better about this is that you will also meet yourself – and that's simply incredible. There's a 2 for 1 deal for ya.

Life is beautiful enough in such a way that allows for us to not have to go on an emotional world tour seeking out the person we want to be with. Nature does some incredible things on its own, free of any help. It grows hundred-foot trees, moves water into the most astonishing waterfalls, shoots stars across night-skies, allows shape-formed snow to fall from clouds, brings together the colors needed to provide a cotton candy sunset, turns a caterpillar into a butterfly, changes seasons, and creates a huge line of colors that seemingly stack on top of one another (without mixing) to form what we call a rainbow. If all this beauty can happen on its own, then the beauty in two souls finding their match can also happen without either of them looking for one another. Finding your soulmate does not need to be forced nor manufactured. They don't even need to be "found". Find the you in you. You'll wind up with much more to contribute beyond yourself. And because you are infinitely beautiful and attractive, you will more than likely become a magnet for the exact person you're longing for and meant to be with.

FINDING YOUR SOULMATE DOES NOT NEED TO BE FORCED NOR MANUFACTURED. THEY DON'T EVEN NEED TO BE "FOUND". FIND THE YOU IN YOU. YOU'LL WIND UP WITH MUCH MORE TO CONTRIBUTE BEYOND YOURSELF. AND BECAUSE YOU ARE INFINITELY BEAUTIFUL AND ATTRACTIVE, YOU WILL MORE THAN LIKELY BECOME A MAGNET FOR THE EXACT PERSON YOU'RE LONGING FOR AND MEANT TO BE WITH.

13

The Importance Of Feeling & Being Alone

L ife plays out in a certain order that most of us share in common. It goes something like: we're born, we're raised by our parent(s) or someone else or some sort of group setting, we go about our teenage years and begin to think for ourselves (or try to) while gaining and losing friends, we become adults and now have our own weight to pull while also trying to figure out what we want to do in life, we work and pursue goals and/or hangout with friends, we partner with someone and reproduce, or we remain alone and continue working, we raise the next generation and/or grow old, then repeat. Obviously, the story is different for everyone, and life is much more complicated than the words I just used to describe it, but we all are somewhere in between the lines above. More importantly, so much is happening to us, around us, and within us, during every phase of our lives. So at what point are we truly, authentically, **intentionally**, and whole-heartedly spending time with ourselves (for ourselves, by ourselves), completely free of distraction?

Let's be clear here: binge-watching Netflix, TV, or Movies while time passes is not spending time with ourselves free of distraction (it may be for some, and I'll break this down further as we continue). A couple of nights, weeks, or years of sleeping alone doesn't exactly qualify for the soul-discovering depth that I am referring to either. Neither does being an orphan, nor being single for a long time, working on a work-related project alone, reading a book alone, etc. Its just not that simple.

The alone time with self that I am speaking of lies in uncomfortable, unfamiliar, untaught places. Paths traveled by few, untraveled by you, sought after by no one that you know, and otherwise indiscoverable to any soul except yours, specifically for your fulfillment. Stick with me here.

One of the most mind-blowing truths in existence to date, is that most people have walked, are walking, or will walk through the entirety of their lives…and never fully discover who they actually are. They might, just might, discover a piece, but rarely tap into the fullness of their being. It is much more common to live out your worst potential, or your average potential, than it is to live out (let alone discover) your full potential. If the former statement is true, then it is also true that it is uncommon to fully learn who you are. Can we change this please? **Give yourself permission to, right now**. Let's start there.

Speaking of starts…studies in early childhood development show that **the quality of our experiences during the first few years of our lives – whether positive or negative – shape how our brains develop**. From birth to age 5, our brains develop more than at any other time of our lives; this has a direct impact on our ability to learn and create the life that we desire. To break this down even further, here's a crazy statistic: 90% of brain growth happens before we even turn 6 years old. AHEM. ***clears throat*** HELLO. THIS MEANS THAT AFTER TURNING 6 YEARS OLD, OUR BRAINS ONLY DEVELOP ABOUT 10% MORE! BY THE TIME WE ARE ADULTS, LET ALONE TEENAGERS, OUR BRAINS HAVE PEAKED IN DEVELOPMENT, WE ACCEPT WHAT WE KNOW TO BE TRUE AND POSSIBLE, AND WE ACCEPT WHAT WE HAVE BECOME.

(credit: firstthingsfirst.org)

Unless we are intentionally proactive about furthering the entirety of our being, we won't. Not to mention, life has presented us with more than enough distraction and 'things' to do, ensuring less and less of a chance and time to reinvent ourselves, develop further, and evolve into greater forms of specimen than we already are. In simpler words, if we do not get serious and active about growing into better versions of ourselves, we will remain so caught up in the day-to-day tasks of living life, that we don't even grow.

Would you take advice on how to create the life of your dreams from a 6 year old? Don't answer that. You already are. We need to spend time with ourselves because there is a 6 year old version in each of us that, in some subtle way, shape, or form, is affecting how we navigate through life. **It is important to re-teach yourself who you are and what you know to be possible, over and over again.** Otherwise, we will remain stagnant as humans. You're not reading this right now because you want to be stagnant. I'm utterly positive that it's quite the opposite – so let's get it.

[To clarify: I know you're not 6 years old – most likely. I know your brain is not 6 years old. The science has simply stated that majority of our *brain development* happens during our early childhood, which shapes the lens in which we see ourselves and the world.]

Now that you're more grown up than 6 year old you, you are your own teacher – or you at least CAN be. You don't have to live or play by anyone else's rules. They don't apply anymore. You can bend them, rewrite them, and reinvent them for yourself! You can discover new boundaries, set new limits, and travel beyond the walls that were put up to keep you safe when you were 6. This is exciting! It's like being able to build your own world from scratch; more realistically, every single day IS an opportunity to RESHAPE our worlds. I can see how this might be riding the very thin line of corniness, but we all have thought about that imaginary restart button where we can press it, go back in time with all that we know now, and start from there. That button is not imaginary. It's real. Right in front of you. It's not even a button. It's the second that you wake up in the morning. It's right now. It's all the time. But if you're too busy doing whatever it is that we do, and you don't intentionally create time to emotionally, spiritually, and energetically *sit with yourself*, you'll completely miss the opportunity – which is known as life. You'll live 100 years with a 6 year old mind.

So what does it look like? Spending time alone, being alone, and feeling alone. Well it's going to be different for everyone. I'm not here to tell you THE way. I'm here to help you find yours. Here's what I can say... **Fear and discomfort are psychological & emotional scents gifted to us in order to help us identify where our boundaries lie. When you pick up on these scents, be curious, and walk towards them.**

Let's say that everything that you know about yourself and your world forms a playground that you live within. Eventually, you'll know the entire playground extremely well. Maybe too well. The slides get old. The monkey bars are no longer high enough for how tall you've grown. And the swings still have the child-proof seats so you can't even sit in them anymore. You've built a house in your area. You're well-off and very comfortable. Just beyond the walls of your playground are things you've never seen, places you've never been, and rumors of even grander playgrounds. Right beside the gate that leads to the other side of the wall surrounding your playground, is a sign that reads "for your own safety, do not exit." But you really don't know why the sign says that or what exactly has been deemed so unsafe. *The playground is you. And your growth & self-identity can only go as far as the boundaries you set and accept for yourself.*

The reality is that most people accept this playground, and the sign on the gate and are completely ok with that. (I am no judge to declare that right or wrong. This particular book is just meant to take you beyond that sign). You see, the stories you've heard and things you were taught, the things you tell yourself, the sounds of wolves and snakes beyond the walls, combined with the fact that you are unable to see what's on the other side of the wall, all make up the sign and the feeling of fear it gives you. Be it fear that you feel, or some other irregular feelings, your boundary is formed by these things.

Very little growth and self-discovery lie between the world you already know, and the things you already know about yourself. The growth and self-discovery that do lie there are limited by your boundaries. I am simply stating that YOU – YOU AS A BEING – AND HOW MUCH YOU CAN GROW, AND HOW MUCH YOU CAN DISCOVER ABOUT YOURSELF IS ACTUALLY *LIMITLESS*. SO WHY STOP? BECAUSE OF SOME SIGN? A sign that you didn't even put up with your own two hands. NO. JUST NO.

Growth and soul-level self discovery are found by following the scent of fear and discomfort. GROWTH AND SOUL-LEVEL SELF DISCOVERY ARE FOUND BY FOLLOWING THE SCENT OF FEAR AND DISCOMFORT. The importance of feeling & being *alone* are in this truth. *Alone* is necessary. Alone – because our fears and areas of discomfort are relative and unique to ourselves. Alone – because you'll learn things about yourself and develop self-awareness free of distraction. Alone – because we, too frequently, lean on others to guide us while we cover our eyes. ***ALONE – BECAUSE WE ARE ACTUALLY MEANT TO BE WITH AND AROUND OTHERS, BUT TOO OFTEN DO SO WITHOUT KNOWLEDGE NOR AWARE-NESS OF WHAT WE ARE CONTRIBUTING TO OR SUBTRACTING FROM THE PEOPLE CLOSEST TO US.*** And lastly, alone – because you don't truly know yourself until you spend time with yourself in uncomfortable and unfamiliar areas of life.

Rather than list examples here, at this point, take a moment to reflect and ask yourself when is the last time you stepped out of your playground, completely alone and free of distraction? When is the last time you did something [consciously and intentionally] by yourself (with yourself, for yourself) that was extremely unfamiliar and uncomfortable for you? **And intentionally, meaning you did so with the intent to learn something new about you, to grow and stretch yourself beyond who you currently are, so that you can be....better**.

The importance here is the following: if you haven't left your current playground yet (the current version of you), then you don't even fully know who you are. Yes, you might know who you are right now, in this current time and place in your life. But challenge yourself to expand what you know about you. In doing so, you will unlock doors in life that you never even knew existed – resulting in a more fulfilled you. How great can you get?

Challenge:

- On a huge piece of paper, draw out a 100-day countdown.
- Date each number.
- Each day, do 1 new thing that you have never done before (listen to a new podcast, read a page of your new book, listen to an album you've never heard, travel, do a new hike, watch a new movie, run a new trail, take a different route, etc).
- For each day that you do 1 new thing, use a green marker to check that day off on the countdown. Write what you did.
- For each day that you do not do 1 new thing, use a red marker to 'x' that day off.
- Keep in mind that the purpose of this is to *expand* yourself. Do things you normally would not. It should feel uncomfortable.

After the 100 days, count how many green days you've had and how many red. Look for patterns. Repeat as many times as you'd like.

THE ALONE TIME WITH SELF THAT I AM SPEAKING OF LIES IN UNCOMFORTABLE, UNFAMILIAR, UNTAUGHT PLACES. PATHS TRAVELED BY FEW, UNTRAVELED BY YOU, SOUGHT AFTER BY NO ONE THAT YOU KNOW, AND OTHERWISE INDISCOVERABLE TO ANY SOUL EXCEPT YOURS, SPECIFICALLY FOR YOUR FULFILLMENT.

14

Stay Single Forever. Let Me Explain...

N ow that I've got your attention, I'll begin with a confession: the title of this chapter is not to be taken literally. Sorry to let the loners of the world down. To clarify, I am not saying to never get into a relationship with someone else. On the contrary, I'm actually saying that no matter what you decide to do or who you decide to date/love/marry/etc – be unshakably sure to continue prioritizing yourself first. To the extremely selfless and big-hearted people out there: don't close the book just yet, it gets better.

If you've ever been on a plane, you're probably familiar with the controversial oxygen mask instructions for emergency procedures, which state that in the event of an emergency, to grab a mask and place it on yourself PRIOR to placing one on a child. Without further thought, this actually sounds mad. Upon further thought, you realize that if you pass out before the child, the child is most likely doomed. There's such a beautiful, underlying principle to this model: if you're not in your best condition, the person who relies on you won't be getting the best version of you. What they will probably be getting is a not-so-good version of you.

For some reason, most people get into relationships and suddenly stop putting on their oxygen mask first! Instead, they start paying more attention to yours, or just don't do anything at all, until the relationship plane crashes. Ok...ok. Enough of the metaphor. You get the point. Relationships are their best when both individuals maintain the qualities that originally made them attractive to the other person in the first place. Put your mask on, we're about to dive deeper.

There are some obvious and not-so-obvious grounds to be covered here. We've all been witness to, maybe even culprit in the sudden stoppage of extremely nice things that were once being done in order to grab the heart of our crush. We've seen the people who suddenly have a change in weight over the course of time, for more reasons than one. We've seen guys lose their six-pack, or the motivation they once had to acquire one. "True colors" seemingly begin to come out of nowhere. That interest they had in reading suddenly declines. That nightly beer before bed turns into a 6-pack before bed. There isn't as much laughter. The two of you don't go out for dinner or to the movies anymore. "I love you" isn't said as much. And the list goes on. I would place these and a lot more in the "obvious" category.

The things above are a byproduct of a truth that happens far too often: clear sight and focus on the things that make you whole are lost as your relationship unfolds and life progresses. Or someone in the *relationship* did not spend enough time alone before taking part in one (see prior chapter titled **The Importance Of Feeling & Being Alone**). This eventually does more harm to the relationship than good. The sound of putting yourself before your partner sounds selfish and probably goes against everything we know to be true about relationships, but that's just the half of it. In sum, **it is of the upmost importance to take care of yourself first, SO THAT you may be better for your partner (or whoever needs you for that matter).** Don't stop doing the things that make you...YOU. It's still selfish – it's just in the "not-so-obvious" category.

Selfishness is a good thing when the end goal is to have a better impact on the people around you. If you're not bringing the best version of you to your relationships, then what are you bringing? The people you care about most are deserving of your best self. Give yourself permission to create time, in the midst of what is required of you in your relationship and life, for the continuous process of leveling up within. This will actually make your relationships and every other part of your life better! **We've got to let go of this false idea that areas of our lives need improvement. When we improve, the areas of our lives do so as a result – including our relationships.**

It is more than okay to have an incredibly huge and giving heart; a heart that serves others before oneself; a caring heart. The truth of the matter is, if we really care about the people around us and special loved ones, then we will prioritize making sure we (you) are in the best position to serve them. I reached a point in my life where I realized I could either keep giving my parents two hundred dollars per week (putting the oxygen mask on them first), or go out into the world and come back a multi-billionaire that provides my parents with whatever it is they need (putting the oxygen mask on myself first). I use this particular example because *Stay Single Forever* does not solely apply to romantic relationships; this principle applies to anyone and anything in your life that you care about. At no point in life, should you completely stop doing as much as you currently can to improve yourself and maintain your best qualities.

In relationships, two WHOLES are required. Getting into relationships with your other *half* sounds cute and romantic, but tread carefully; you may find yourself putting in extra effort to fill someone's cup, which ultimately drains you. Or you may be on the other end of this, bringing your half-full cup to the relationship, and draining the person you love right out of your life. **This is not an anti-going-through-things-together chapter. This is a pro-grow-within-so-**

that-you-don't-drown-your-loved-ones-while-they're-trying-to-rescue-you chapter. People enjoy helping those who help themselves. The same way lovers love loving people who love themselves. Read that again.

Let's keep tapping into truth here; this book is not for the shallow. Someone can only love you (and you be receptive of it) as much as you love yourself. Ever hear of emotional-unavailability? It's a real thing. It's when you don't let someone in. Typically that "someone" genuinely wants to love you in ways you have probably never experienced, and because you're emotionally unavailable, they are unable to. We tend to enter this emotional space after being hurt. Someone breaks our heart, and we hire *emotional security guards* that exist in our heads to protect us. «« THIS IS NOT LOVING YOURSELF. Loving yourself requires forgiving yourself and others, and then setting the intent to not allow previous experiences to shape how available you'll be in experiences to come. Some will spend a lifetime in this emotional space (of not loving oneself), which will be draining for whoever comes along with plenty of love to give. ***Stay Single Forever*** means taking care of your emotional space, tending to it, nurturing it, maturing it, and healing it; ***Stay Single Forever*** does not mean place the emotional security guards in front of the gates of your heart & feelings.

What have you grown to love about yourself while being alone? What things did you when you were single that ignited the YOU in YOU? What is it that fans the fuel within your spirit? What do you do for fun? DO NOT STOP DOING THESE THINGS JUST BECAUSE YOU'RE IN A RELATIONSHIP (unless they are harmful to your partner). As long as it doesn't compromise your integrity, nor the trust your partner has in you, and your grandma would be proud...go for it.

*[Note to partner: aim to be in a place where you can give your significant other permission to be 100% selfish when they need to be, with trust that it is for the betterment of themselves and the relationship. (More on this in **How***

To Make Your Relationship Last Forever)]

I am, personally, very intentional about communicating the freedom, permission, and support my Queen has to be 100% selfish whenever she needs to be. This can present itself in ways as simple as a spa day, booking a staycation at a cool hotel for herself, and going to the movies alone; or it can be deeper things involving her career, aspirations, or hobbies that I do not share – either way, I want her to send it! Her being in a healthy relationship with herself is of greater priority to me, than anything involving the two of us. I understand that my supporting her to **Stay Single Forever** actually strengthens our togetherness. My trust in all we keep sacred is solidified by my dating a WHOLE person, and vice versa.

Stay Single Forever encourages an indulgence in something consistent with the purpose of this book: a better you. No matter how big of a heart one has, or how great of a lover you are, the best way to go about expressing those things START with maintaining them. **Do your daily inner-maintenance so that your being may be a temple of love for your soulmate and people you keep close to heart**. Failure to maintain, nurture, and grow the best inner-you possible, leaves room for falling apart – and you are just too damn necessary to allow such a thing. Stay single. Stay connected.

STAY SINGLE FOREVER MEANS TAKING CARE OF YOUR EMOTIONAL SPACE, TENDING TO IT, NURTURING IT, MATURING IT, AND HEALING IT; STAY SINGLE FOREVER DOES NOT MEAN PLACE THE EMOTIONAL SECURITY GUARDS IN FRONT OF THE GATES OF YOUR HEART + FEELINGS.

15

How To Make Your Relationship Last For An Eternity. And Why Most Don't.

[Disclaimer: reading this chapter will not make your relationship last forever. Only you have the power to do that. The following words are merely a guide of measures you can take to help bring out the best in your relationship. This chapter was written from a place of love, before experience and observation. This chapter also does not give a how-to manual for finding the person you want to be in a relationship with – that subject is touched on in the chapters 12 & 13.

I once heard an incredible lady ask a question. It was something along the lines of "why is it that when it comes to our careers, crafts, passions, projects, education and more…we spend hours, days, weeks, months, years, and decades studying or practicing those things to the point of mastery…yet we don't put that same type of energy, effort, and time into studying our partners?" A simpler version of this question would be something like "why does the surfer practice surfing for 10 hours a day, while his spouse only gets 1 hour of Netflix a day?" Read this paragraph again – these are the types of questions that never get asked, but we'll address them here.

Realistically, most of us will not put an equal amount of time into our relationships as we do practicing & mastering our careers, crafts, passions, projects, education and more – and you should not be expected to (it would be nice, but you shouldn't be expected to). However, this isn't even about an *equal* amount of time. The question above does put things into perspective by using time as a variable, but it's the *principle* behind the question that we are here to discuss. If it takes hours, days, weeks, months, years, and decades of practicing/studying something in order to know it/perform it at the point of mastery, why would the same principle not apply to knowing your spouse and growing your relationship? Think about this for a minute.

It is all too common that people get into relationships, and then NOT work on the relationship. We are not studying our loved ones enough. We spend time doing things together, sure, but we don't lock ourselves in a room and write down important notes about our spouses on index cards until the point of memory. We are not learning and actively seeking out their love languages and then practicing different ways of communicating those to them. We are not failing and then trying to reexplore completely different angles of their being. We don't know the depths of their soul. We aren't watering the parts of them that are deeply rooted in the life THEY want to create. We aren't active and intentional about getting constructive feedback from them about how we can be better for them. We are not allowing them to be the teacher of themselves. We aren't the best students of them that we can be. We hear only what they communicate at surface level, instead of their truth. We haven't even broken a sweat yet. We think we have, because we've been doing what WE know and think to be effective, instead of seeking that from *within them.*

One of the most disappointing truths about relationships is that their entirety can be spent loving someone in ways that they do not want nor need to be loved. I have seen people use their financial stability, and ability to provide, as a way of communicating the love they have inside, all the while their spouse does not receive love in that manner. People have spent years of energy arguing how hard they are trying to or have tried to make things work, all the while their spouse says they've done *nothing* at all. People have dedicated the entirety of their careers and time spent at work to providing a better life for their family, all the while their spouse feels none of it. There's something to be said about this disconnect...

Not only is this clear cut evidence of the fact that we have not spent enough time learning our significant other, it also further emphasizes the importance of making sure that we do! After the movies have finished, the dinner dates have concluded, we've gotten comfortable enough to fart around one another, we've moved in together, and have plans on creating a life together, THERE IS STILL LOTS OF SOUL-LEVEL EXPLORING TO BE DONE. It takes about 10 years of active studying in order to BECOME a doctor, and that's just the starting point. Best believe and deeply understand that it takes no less to learn another human being in the ways that a relationship require, and that is also just the start.

[*I am not saying that you must stay in a relationship for 10 years in order to know your significant other.* **It's not the time, it's the level of work, energy, effort, drive, desire, passion, dedication, and unshakable love for whatever it is that you do. THAT is what we're tapping into in this chapter. THAT (*learning the love receptors of your spouse*) should MATCH, IF NOT OUTWEIGH, what you're putting into your craft/career or any other area of your life.** *This truth furthers the importance of being with someone you're willing to do that for.*]

The truth of the matter is no chapter in any book is going to give you the secret to make your relationship last forever. What you will leave with from this chapter however, are tools and knowledge that can bring *yours* near the point of bulletproof, if applied. One of the most valuable keys to life lie in the *way* that we word our questions. Let's start with this one: "What are 2-3 things that I can do to improve myself?" The BEAUTIFUL, underlying music to this question will be heard in the answer you get from the person you ask. It is said that when people give advice, a major part of what they say stems from their own perspective & experiences, and not yours. That's precisely the goal of this question. By asking your significant other this question a few times a year, or whenever you want for that matter, you are more than likely pulling out an answer that comes from what THEY need from you, rather than what you need for you. It's subtle, but effective. To coat it a bit more, and make it easier to answer, tell them to also give you 2-3 things that you do really well on top of that. They will spill the beans. [*The reason why the question is not "what are 2-3 things that I can do to be better for you/our relationship?" is because phrasing it that way threatens the psychological safety of the answer. They will most likely think of their own faults in the relationship, and then feel too unsafe to point out yours. By phrasing the question in a more general space, you allow for a more comfortable answer.*]

What is psychological safety? Super glad you asked. It's arguably the most important factor and driving force of success for ANY and every genuine connection; be it relationships, friendships, companies, etc. Without it, a huge piece goes missing – authentic self. And when authentic self is missing from any type of connection, the success and growth of that connection is limited. **PSYCHOLOGICAL SAFETY IS THE SAFE SPACE THAT IS INTENTIONALLY, PURPOSEFULLY, CONSCIOUSLY, AND PERPETUALLY <u>CREATED & MOLDED</u> IN ORDER TO ALLOW FOR 100% PERMISSION TO BE ONE'S AUTHENTIC SELF.** Think of your closest friend - that's probably someone who you have naturally reaped the benefits of psychological safety with. In relationships, this is developed naturally over time for most of us, yes, but as the relationship goes on, psychological safety must be ***proactively*** enforced! We have to be intentional about this thing, or we risk it fading away. Ask yourself "what are some ways I can get creative about making sure my loved one feels like they can communicate anything and everything to me?" **Simply thinking like this** will place you in a position, mentally, to learn more about your significant other. When the both of you are asking yourselves this type of question...you're in for one lit relationship.

The goal here is to forever bring out the authentic-self in your partner. You have the ability to think of so many different ways to go about doing so. And as you do, you'll uncover new layers of your soulmate to fall in love with. This is actually a lot of fun. Just because you think you know everything about them, doesn't mean that's necessarily true. Studies have shown that the average human brain has an estimated 60,000 to 80,000 thoughts per day. You probably share no more than 10 of them, if the people around you are lucky. I try to get at least 100 of them out of my Queen, and closest friends.

[If you think you know your partner, or anyone else for that matter, consider this: they have almost 80,000 thoughts per day. You'd be lucky to have more than 3 of those shared with you – I mean, be honest...how many do you share? Mind you, 3 thoughts out of 80,000 is less than 1% of their thoughts. It might take 80,000 days to have 80,000 thoughts shared with you. Just to put that into perspective...80,000 days = 219 years. Meaning it's more than likely we will go our entire lifetime without TRULY knowing our partner / it could take more than 2 lifetimes to truly get to know our partner, or anyone else! You've got some exploring to do...]

Allow me to share something a bit more personal, just to provide an example of how I exercise the principles being discussed in this chapter. My girlfriend would absolutely love to journal every single morning...in an ideal world. She's working on being more consistent with it, but struggles for more reasons than one. This is so important because she has an estimated 160,000 thoughts per day, which is double the average brain. (This is just my opinion on the matter, based on observation. It may or may not be an accurate number) When she doesn't get these thoughts out, Godzilla comes out instead, and I'm like "Rex" from Toy Story. I asked myself how I could add value to her, in regard to getting her thoughts out, while also bringing something new to our relationship. What I came up with is now known as our 'coffee and a walk'. This is simply a daily walk that we take in the mornings, prior to giving ourselves to the day and all that is required of us. One of us makes the pot of coffee, we throw on a sweatshirt & flip flops, and head out for a walk to wherever our conversation takes us. I made sure to communicate with her that these walks are not only an opportunity for us to spend time together before our days start, but more importantly, that "coffee and a walk" is a non-judgement zone, a time for us to speak on anything no matter how dark or exciting, and a time for her to be heard without advice-like responses unless she wants one. I could go on for hours about the psychological safety that these walks have opened up for our relationship, but hopefully this paragraph suffices. I am amazed, not only at how much I've learned about her during these mornings, but also at the impact that it has had on her attitude, productivity, and perspective – she is much more at peace. I have seen rare sightings of Godzilla. The best part is that we've made it a non-negotiable...for the most part. No matter the day, whether we are together or apart, or how late we might have woken up – we aim to make this happen.

Not only has "coffee and a walk" watered our relationship, more importantly, it has watered her, and been a form of journaling. The only difference is I am her diary now. THAT is JUST ONE of the ways we have gone about actively working on our relationship, while being intentional about bringing out the authentic-self in one another. I simply encourage you to do the same. Whether it be "coffee and a walk" or something even more genius that you come up with...explore this territory of your relationship. **Psychological safety** may not be THE sole factor of making your relationship last forever, but it is undoubtedly THE start, and inarguably a necessity for the success of each and every connection that exists. Go make yours last forever.

THE GOAL HERE IS TO FOREVER BRING OUT THE AUTHENTIC-SELF IN YOUR PARTNER. YOU HAVE THE ABILITY TO THINK OF SO MANY DIFFERENT WAYS TO GO ABOUT DOING SO. AND AS YOU DO, YOU'LL UNCOVER NEW LAYERS OF YOUR SOULMATE TO FALL IN LOVE WITH. THIS IS ACTUALLY A LOT OF FUN.

16

Let's Talk About Love Though

S o so happy to be here. Here as in this chapter. The title holds the exact words I'd like to scream at the nominees during a U.S. political debate. It's just a little something I like to imagine every now and then, but I truly do wonder how they'd respond. How would you? I mean, so many other topics quickly and easily ignite conversation; like sports, the Kardashians, plans for this weekend, TV shows, movies, racism, climate change, finances, our jobs, schoolwork, our lives in general, etc. But what about _love_? What's your take on it? How well do you understand it? What's your experience with it? And when is the last time you talked about it? Let alone thought about it. I know for me personally, it's thought about almost every day. It has _that_ level of importance for me, and the ways I use it in my life. It's our superpower – which is why I strongly believe that we need to push the conversation around it more.

It's challenging to think about where to start when it comes to this topic, but allow me to begin with what I mean by 'superpower'. Try to think of any superhero in one of the movies or shows you've seen. The special things they do are most commonly known as _superpowers,_ but those special things are really just gifts, talents, and abilities. **A superpower is the highest degree of capability to do or accomplish something**. Really, that's what a superpower is. *Dictionary.com* defines **super** (adjective) as "of the highest degree"; and **power** (noun) as the "capability of doing or accomplishing something". So there you have it – this isn't just my opinion! It's official! What does this have to do with love? I'm getting there. Don't rush me.

Look, if you're reading this book cover to cover then you probably guessed by now that I'm about to tell you that <u>you have superpowers</u>; but please do not take this lightly. Not right now. Not in this chapter. I am more specifically saying that **YOU HAVE THE HIGHEST DEGREE OF CAPABILITY TO DO OR ACCOMPLISH SOME-THING**. [*Read that aloud to run it through your subconscious one time.*] **I HAVE THE HIGHEST DEGREE OF CAPABILITY TO DO OR ACCOMPLISH SOMETHING**. That *something* is not only infinite, but also completely up to you. When *love* is applied to your superpower (your highest degree of capability to accomplish something), your gifts, talents, and abilities not only reveal themselves, but also show out in ways that far exceed the ordinary – and this is what superheroes do. You have a choice of what to do with your superpower. I will push the conversation of love from out of this truth. Let's go for a walk…

We've seen definitions of love. We've heard others' definitions of love. We've witnessed science attempting to define & understand it. However, we've barely tapped into it as a human race. The exploration of love (as a human race) has been great, but we've fallen short mainly because we're seeking it out from a finite lens, rather than an infinite lens. We've been more interested in defining love, than we are in exploring the heights and depths of it – and what we can do with it. Even with what interest we've expressed in it as a whole, it's still no where near enough. Evidence of this openly, easily, and clearly identifies itself in the fact that we are thousands of years into our existence and yet still dealing with wars, racism, classism, vengeance, grudges, unforgiveness, oppression, systemic oppression, abuse, dishonesty, unwillingness to understand, selfishness, greed, rape, inequality, murder, injustice…I mean, we could go on but you get it. I hope you get it. Stick with me here…

The extraordinary things mentioned above – yes, they're on the bad side of extraordinary, but they are by no means ordinary – are only possible because they have a channel in which they are able to manifest themselves through: *superpowers*. All of these bad things are being done by people exercising their *highest degree of capability to accomplish* them. [*Read that back once more.*] So I repeat, when LOVE is applied to your superpower (your highest degree of capability to accomplish something), your gifts, talents, and abilities not only reveal themselves, but also show out in ways that far exceed the ordinary. What are you applying to your superpower? Is it doubt? Is it hate? Is it fear? Is it confidence? Is it love? Tread carefully, because what you choose to apply to your superpower has a direct impact on the outcome of your 'something'. Remember **you have the highest degree of capability to do or accomplish 'something'**. You may not be doing all of the evil things mentioned above, but are you holding a grudge? Are you unforgiving about something that happened to you in your life? Are you being dishonest about certain things? Or are you just trying to maintain and live a low-key life until you die? Are you settling for mediocrity in your life? Are you accepting things as they are and telling yourself you *can't* change them? YOU ARE DOING 'SOMETHING' AT YOUR HIGHEST DEGREE OF CAPABILITY – even if it's failing, doing nothing at all, or just getting by. If you are doing good with your superpower – awesome. Let's lean into how to be even greater through LOVE.

I'm not here to tell you the meaning of love. I don't even believe it has a 'meaning'. I believe it has infinite meanings that we may or may not even be meant to uncover in full. Loving another being such as a family member, significant other, or friend, has seemingly been where we have peaked (in regard to love). We have so much more of it to explore and put to use within our superpower. This chapter simply serves as a means to start the conversation. *You* carry it farther. Carry it out into all aspects of your life and into your superpower (again...*your highest degree of capability to do or accomplish something*).

When we think of the greatest athletes of all time, people like Serena Williams, Michael Jordan, Kobe Bryant, Michael Phelps, Tiger Woods, Mia Hamm, Billie Jean King, Cristiano Ronaldo, Lionel Messi, Ronda Rousey, Danika Patrick, Lebron James, and the list goes on...we think of gifts, talents, and abilities on steroids! Not literally on steroids, but these people are performing (or have performed) the exact same sport as their peers yet execute at a level far beyond the ordinary. What do we attribute this to? On the obvious side lies hard work, practice, maybe being athletically-inclined, time, drive, passion, etc. But the *less talked-about* factor in play here is LOVE. I acknowledge that a lot goes into what makes these athletes great. However, I believe that what we've seen from these people is what happens when *love* has a host to exercise it's strength through. **The greater the work put in, the greater the athlete – sure. But the greater the love, the greater the willingness and commitment to put the work in**. If you look closely enough, there is a clear connection and correlation between one's performance and one's **love** for what is being performed. Athletes are just ONE example of the effect that love can have. **Love can take an ordinary thing to extraordinary heights. It can take a relationship to marriage. It can turn a selfish person into an amazing parent. It can take average performance to outstanding performance. What are you doing with it?**

Given the sacrifices I've seen a mother make for her child (even mine for me), the businesses we've seen built from nothing, the athletes we've seen come from homeless to setting the peak in their given fields, the feelings that arise within us because of another human being, the work ethic and drive of people doing things that most never will, the level of attachment we are capable of developing, the amount of giving and contribution to others beyond measure, the charitable foundations that have been built by people who endured long-suffering, and so much more... it has become more and more evidently clear that *love* is capable of driving us places far beyond the imaginable. There are too many things we have done that were once considered impossible, too many feats we have accomplished that were once deemed improbable, too great of people we have become out of the darkest of circumstances – and behind EACH is a **LOVE** for something or someone. It is that love – that level of muscle – that has ultimately propelled us.

If there is something that you want to do, or a version of yourself that you want to be, the very first means of manifesting that should be LOVE. Look what it's done! If it doesn't exist in what you're doing, or who you're becoming, to what extent can the extraordinary occur? With it, to what degree of infinity can you go? You can be the Michael Phelps of life's troubled waters, but you've got to LOVE first yourself, then where you're headed. You might be able to get by without it, but that's not why you're reading this book. You're here because there is a love inside you that is screaming for something greater to latch onto, so that you can exercise your superpowers. Maybe you've already found it, maybe not. *Love* doesn't care whether you have or not. It's still equally accessible to all – it is birthed within us! Seek this thing out! Don't let the greatest muscle inside of you go to waste. Exercise it in all that you do. It does not run out. It can stretch as far as you're willing to go, and it can feed your willingness when paired with the right 'something'.

Whatever lack of fulfillment that exists in what you've done, what you're doing, who you are, or who you're becoming, is more than likely evidence of the lack of LOVE you have for it. [*Read that again;*

103

it's spot on.] **IF YOU DO NOT FEEL FULFILLMENT IN WHAT YOU'VE DONE, WHAT YOU'RE DOING, WHO YOU ARE, OR WHO YOU'RE BECOMING – YOU PROBABLY DON'T LOVE IT. IF YOU DON'T LOVE IT, IT WILL NOT BE SUSTAINABLY & GENUINELY EXTRAORDINARY.**

The word 'fulfillment' is used above with much intent. Fulfillment speaks to the **process** behind your *something,* more than the result. You can be, and ideally should be, extremely fulfilled by what you're doing and who you're becoming long before the 'success' comes. Fulfillment will be felt almost the entire time when you truly love something, even on the off days - especially when you love yourself.

So now my question to you is... *If you can be extraordinary and do extraordinary things by simply LOVING who you're becoming or what you're doing, why would you spend time being someone or doing something that you don't love?* That would ultimately be synonymous with accepting ordinary, and more dangerously, not being in alignment with LOVE – the greatest muscle of all.

So how do we tap into it? Well, *You Name It*. I'll give some of the ways I go about implementing love into all that I do, say, and think; but ultimately, YOU will better YOUR being and YOUR life by seeking out YOUR own unique ways to BE LOVE and channel it into all you do, say, and think. The best part is that this isn't too difficult. It does take lots of practice and application (consistency), but over time, you will notice a difference in your conversations, emotions, relationships, goals, etc.

Here's one of the basic ways I go about utilizing love as a means of having a fulfilling experience: I live in a house with 4 other roommates; none of which enjoy doing the dishes as much as I *seem* to. It's going on four years now that I have been living with this amount of people, so you can imagine, or relate to, what a sink full of 5 people's dishes look like. A few months ago, one of my roommates took the initiative to wash a sink full of dishes. She did so…well…let's say…aggressively. She blurted out some not-so-nice words as she was doing them. I responded by saying "if you're not going to do the dishes with love, then don't do them. It's not worth it for you just to get upset. I'll do them – I don't mind." That didn't stop her from playing the tambourine with the house plates. But who does dishes with "love" anyways? This guy.

I don't actually enjoy washing dishes. No one does. But long ago I stopped stressing over my other roommates not doing them. Here's why… I realized that I do not like walking into a kitchen, ready to cook a *fire* meal, only to be faced with a sink full of the dishes that I need to use. I also just really like living in a clean space. So I thought to myself, if I don't like a sink full of dishes, my roommates probably don't either. If I would like a clean kitchen to cook in, then my roommates would probably like the same. I want my roommates to enjoy living with me, and they are deserving of a clean kitchen, so I took it upon myself to embrace the responsibility of doing the dishes and keeping the kitchen clean for everyone to use. Did this change the fact that no one else did the dishes? Ehh. But being LOVING made me a better, more compassionate person. It made me more patient, more caring, and most importantly eliminated the stress associated with dishes and roommates who don't wash them. Now, each time that I wash the dishes, no matter how full the sink is, I have positive thoughts associated with it: I love my roommates, I love a clean kitchen, and my roommates deserve a clean kitchen the same way I do – I don't want anyone to have to walk into a dirty kitchen.

Look, I'm aware of how lame this might sound right now. But it's still true. **By simply thinking and operating from a place of LOVE, I turned a frustrating and meaningless chore into a way to practice bettering myself. If I can do this with dishes, imagine what more you can do with much greater hurdles in your life.**

Here's one more example of how I exercise the use LOVE in my life…
I'd say ever since I became a teenager, my mom and I have argued about
almost anything capable of being argued: dishes, going to church, bills,
cleaning my room, family issues, where I'm going, who I'm hanging out
with, and the list goes on. I now live on the other side of the country
from her, and we've even found things to argue about on the phone
while 3,000 miles apart. I recently made a shift in the way I talk to *and*
with her. I now ask myself "Am I listening from a place of love?" and
"Am I speaking from a place of love?" – and this small change has made
all the difference. This shifts our conversations from shouting debates
to civil communication. As a result, I have become an even greater
communicator – aka a better me!

Corny? Potentially. True? Absolutely. In this chapter, we've touched
on how LOVE has impacted the performance of the greatest athletes
walking the planet, and how LOVE has impacted my ability to do dishes
stress-free and not yell at my mom. If you still do not see the potential
that LOVE has in your life when you apply it to ANYTHING (even
dishes), then allow me to clarify…

You. Have. Super. Powers. [insert power-claps while reading
those words] **Meaning you have the highest degree of capability
to do 'something' (aka whatever you choose to). When you
apply LOVE to your *something*, whether it be dishes, not yelling
at your mom, communicating with people, expressing yourself, playing a sport, forgiving someone, opening a business,
excelling in school, growing your career, bettering your relationship, being a better you, etc… YOU WILL ACHIEVE THE EX-
TRAORDINARY. Why? Because LOVE IS EXTRAORDINARY.
ANYTHING LOVE TOUCHES BECOMES EXTRAORDINARY –
INCLUDING YOUR FULFILLMENT.**

Love. Love. LOVE. When we really tap into this thing, we will
continue to witness what extraordinary things we're capable of.

Moving forward, ask yourself, in all that you do, "Am I operating out of a place of love?" "Am I conversing out of a place of love?" "Am I responding out of love?" "Am I learning out of love?" If the answer is anything short of yes, ask "Who do I need to be, in order to operate from a place of love?" A great way to begin practicing the use of love in your life is by seeking opportunities to. Simply ask… "How can I?" Guess where I wrote this book from a place of? Love.

THERE ARE TOO MANY THINGS WE HAVE DONE THAT WERE ONCE CONSIDERED IMPOSSIBLE, TOO MANY FEATS WE HAVE ACCOMPLISHED THAT WERE ONCE DEEMED IMPROBABLE, TOO GREAT OF PEOPLE WE HAVE BECOME OUT OF THE DARKEST OF CIRCUMSTANCES – AND BEHIND EACH IS A LOVE FOR SOMETHING OR SOMEONE. IT IS THAT LOVE – THAT LEVEL OF MUSCLE – THAT HAS ULTIMATELY PROPELLED US.

17

There Is No Right Or Wrong Way

Which route you take is not as important as the person you are when making the decision, or who you become along the route. We use the words 'right' and 'wrong' too liberally, as if there is a rule book somewhere for our life decisions. This is simply not the case.

An interesting fact most people don't know is that Elon Musk's father insisted he go to college in Pretoria, but Elon decided to go to college in the United States. Was Elon's father wrong? Was Elon right? Doesn't matter. What matters is that Elon Musk made the decision that was closest to his heart. And look where he is today. There is an unspoken level of intuition in this particular scenario that probably won't be mentioned in stories of Elon Musk's early life. However, this is the goal – to know ourselves at our core well enough to follow what our TRUE selves want to do. Deciding to do otherwise does not make us wrong, it simply limits what we are capable of – and whether that is right or wrong is up to you and what you want out of this life.

Concern about an outcome is natural. We would all love to ensure that on the other side of every decision we make lie our best interest. However, it may not be in our best interest to over-stress and judge ourselves for every decision we make, made, or are about to make. "Did I make the right choice?" and "Am I making the right choice?" are surface level questions that distract us from what our hearts are really asking – which is "Did you listen to me?" or "Are you listening to me?" and "Are you choosing the decision closest to me?" Often times, emotion and intuition can be just as valuable as logic, if not more. You become truly dangerous when you align all three – emotion, intuition, and logic. The uneasy feeling we have when faced with difficult decisions is usually a result of disharmony between these three things.

There is no right or wrong way, but either way, the way is *yours*. 'Right' and 'wrong' are words that we often times associate with outcomes. And as we discuss in the chapter '**Mountains Are The Means. The Man Is The End. Mount Everest.**', outcomes have been misplaced in our line of focus – which leads to disempowerment. YOU are the way. The focus is better placed on **YOU** for the simple fact that when you operate from a place of inner alignment & connectivity, you tend to make decisions that are best for your overall being and soul. When we operate from a place of distraction, doubt, and internal chaos, we tend to make decisions that are attached to a desired outcome which may or may not happen.

In sum, what we are getting at in this chapter is: **inner work leads to higher quality decision making and choices**. If you *find yourself* questioning whether you're on the right path or not, be glad that you found yourself! It is here that you must dig past that surface level question and seek out what it is within you that you are uncertain about. Uncertainty within leads to uncertainty on the outside. Ironically, certainty has long been considered one of our human needs. Please allow me to be the first to tell you that **the further you search within, the more depth you will find; and the more depth that you find within, the more sure of YOURSELF you will be**. In my experience, this journey has led me to a place of very little worry or concern about my past, where I currently am, or the future – because I AM CERTAIN THAT I AM DOING MY ABSOLUTE BEST [WITHIN] RIGHT HERE IN THIS MOMENT. It is because of this truth, that I am CERTAIN I will be fulfilled no matter the outcome of my circumstances, goals, and life. That truth is the same for me day in and day out. Inner work can be an *unshakeable controllable* in your life when you face it and allow it to be. **Let your desired outcome be inner work, rather than the right [or wrong] path.**

Repeat this affirmation daily: I HAVE VERY LITTLE WORRY OR CONCERN ABOUT MY PAST, WHERE I CURRENTLY AM, AND THE FUTURE – BECAUSE I AM CERTAIN THAT I AM DOING MY ABSOLUTE BEST [WITHIN] RIGHT HERE IN THIS MOMENT. IT IS BECAUSE OF THIS TRUTH, THAT I AM CERTAIN I AM FULFILLED NO MATTER THE OUTCOME OF MY CIRCUMSTANCES, GOALS, AND LIFE. THAT TRUTH IS THE SAME FOR ME DAY IN AND DAY OUT. MY DESIRED OUTCOME IS INNER WORK. I AM MY PATH.

OFTEN TIMES, EMOTION AND INTUITION CAN BE JUST AS VALUABLE AS LOGIC, IF NOT MORE. YOU BECOME TRULY DANGEROUS WHEN YOU ALIGN ALL THREE – EMOTION, INTUITION, AND LOGIC.

18

Urgent vs. Important

Yes, there is a difference, and it's not a small one. We're not talking dictionary definitions either; we are tapping into life-impacting differentiation. We are complex. We all have a lot going on. And all of it has to get done somehow, some way, and at some point. But what comes first? What goes last? Do the laundry now? Or go workout? Let's talk about it...

One of the greatest reasons for our inefficiencies and shortcomings is lacking peace of mind. *Peace of mind* meaning being okay with what is in front of us and how we are going to deal with it. It's all too common that we wake up with a to-do list for the day and get little to none of it done due to feeling overwhelmed by the list in its entirety. We daydream instead. Or just lay there thinking of what we're going to do, for so long that more time passes than we've realized, and then it's too late because something else has come up or something else is required of us. This stops now. Moving forward, let's break our to-do lists into two categories: urgent and important.

Urgent things are the things that are in our face now, need to get done asap, or else poop will seemingly hit the fan pretty soon. These are things like laundry, responding to messages/emails, being on time to

113

work/school, doing the dishes, cleaning our rooms/houses/apartments, eating, walking the dog, not missing the game/tv episode, getting things organized, being on time for the event/party/meeting, taking the garbage out, meeting that deadline, etc., **YOU NAME IT**. These are all mainly time-sensitive, and if they don't get done soon, things get ugly. Cool.

Important things are the things that we truly and wholeheartedly want to be or know we should be doing. These are things like meditating, answering the phone when mom/dad calls, stretching/yoga in the morning, journaling, writing down affirmations, reading, planning out our finances, visualizing the life we wish to create, MAKING/CREATING time, putting things into our calendar, calling that close friend you've been thinking about, starting that business you've been wanting to, running that marathon you've been avoiding, going to the gym, working out, spending time with the kids, spending time with the significant other, writing that book you've been wanting to, signing up for that volunteer role you've been thinking about, traveling, quitting your job that you hate, etc., **YOU NAME IT**. These are typically NOT time-sensitive. If they don't get done today, we can just do them tomorrow, or the day after, or the day after that, or on Monday, or next year; maybe even never, and we'll be okay. Nothing will hit the fan if these things don't get done soon. So we focus on and prioritize the urgent instead, and IF we have time (not create/make time), then and only then will we do the important things.

Let me be the first to tell you that you can absolutely go about life this way and be just fine. You can absolutely put the urgent things first and do the important things later. You might become very successful this way. You might make a lot of money. You can. You can. You can. But let me also tell you that you will only be *just fine*. Your soul won't have the fulfillment that you truly desire. You won't connect with others beyond the surface. You won't connect with yourself beyond

114

your surface. You won't learn who you truly are. And you won't tap into your full potential. You'll just be super organized and the kind of person that gets [urgent] things done. Cool.

My guess is you're the kind of person who wants that, yes, but also wants more. That's why we're here right now, reading this book isn't it? In some way, shape, or form, you believe you're capable of more, and you want it. You want a better life, a better you, and better experiences. *You*. Have. To. Come. First. [Insert more claps in between those words.] Any and every task [outside of the task that is yourself] is a distraction FROM yourself. Your comfort zone LOVES this truth. That is why it is so incredibly easy to put the growth and betterment of yourself off until you finish the urgent stuff first. The comfort zone within each of us says we'll "just do that later" (tomorrow, or some other day/time in the future). **The comfort zone in you realizes that if you begin focusing on yourself and doing the things that you truly and whole-heartedly want to do, your life will change, and you won't be the same person anymore. To a comfort zone, that is scary!** If your life changes, and you outgrow your current habits and ways of thinking and operating, then the current you doesn't get to ride along. The current version of you doesn't like that. You ultimately kill off this version of you, that you created in the first place – and that is not an easy task. So in order to slow this process down, the brain will amplify the degree of urgency of tasks around you on a day to day basis. If left up to who you are right now, your being would ultimately be JUST FINE if you stayed the same. But **THE REAL YOU at the inner most part of your core, seeks to evolve, level up, and blossom beyond the current life you have created for yourself**. Proof of that lies in the fact that you're reading these words right now. So let's take you there.

If there is any part of you telling yourself that your improvement and inner-work should not, in fact, come first before any and every thing

– it is a lie. **You** should be THE priority in your life because any and every thing in and around your life is an extension of you. Prioritize yourself by taking care of what is *important* to you first. Change your life by taking care of the urgent things...*as a better version of you*. Trust...**the urgent things in your life are not going anywhere; they will be there when you're done taking care of yourself first**. The important things in your life, however, are different altogether. The impact of neglecting what is important to you, does not lie in the uncertainty that they will disappear, but rather in the certainty that **YOU** will disappear in the chaos of doing urgent things for the rest of your life. Don't let *you* disappear. What is important to you? What is urgent? Important first. Urgent after.

Fill up these circles with your things!

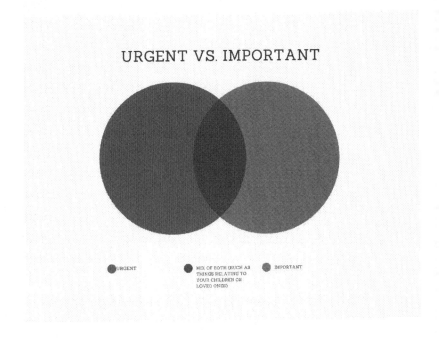

116

THE COMFORT ZONE IN YOU REALIZES THAT IF YOU BEGIN FOCUSING ON YOURSELF AND DOING THE THINGS THAT YOU TRULY AND WHOLE-HEARTEDLY WANT TO DO, YOUR LIFE WILL CHANGE, AND YOU WON'T BE THE SAME PERSON ANYMORE. TO A COMFORT ZONE, THAT IS SCARY!

19

Stress, Anxiety, Depression – What They Really Mean And Why You're Going Growing Through It

Allow me to begin this chapter by stating that stress, anxiety, and depression are VERY real things. The side of society that does not experience or has not experienced the peak effects of these takeovers will fall short each and every time when trying to relate. Some simply won't get 'it'. I intentionally use the word 'takeovers' because stress, anxiety, and depression in their strongest forms truly do *take over* our being; **also because anything that has been taken over can be taken back**. If you've dealt with any of these, then you are very much aware of the utterly paralyzing effect they can have. And I mean *paralyzing* – to the point where you not only mentally, but also physically feel incapable of moving or doing anything. You pass the point of wanting to give up. You pass the point of panic, to the point where you're immobile; and you feel completely disconnected from everyone around. The weight of your problems are at an all-time high. You don't see how you're going to be okay 10 minutes from now. Nothing else matters except for what is in front of you – that being the instant shock and realization of your current reality – which is that everything is not okay, you're not okay, and there is no yellow brick road leading you out of this dark place. You're actually farther than you've ever been from where you want to be. Farther than ever from yourself. On top of all of that, no one can help. No one understands. Life is not slowing down to give you a break. And your heart & mind are literally going to explode any moment now.

For some, the above is a daily reality. For others, it's once in a while. Let me be the first to tell you that you are not alone, you are understood, you are experiencing something legitimate, and most importantly, you are capable of growing through it. I say that from personal experience. **I also say 'grow' through it rather than 'go' through it because empowerment is just more fun**. But in order to grow through something, we have to dig to the root of it, and explore the core of it.

It is not your fault that you are dealing with, or have dealt with stress, anxiety, or depression. Read that back once more before reading any further. It is a crucial truth to understand and accept. **As true as it is, that these things can impair our ability to function, we do not end here. You know that, and that is why you're still alive, breathing**, and reading this book. You still have a lot more left inside of you. More hope. More good. More power. You also know that it's your *responsibility* to overcome your stress, anxiety, and depression. So, how do we? Well, *You Name It*. What that means is that you are going to overcome what you're going through **in your own way**. What you will leave here with, is an understanding of what these things are, what they mean, and why you're ~~going~~ growing through them. Let this chapter serve as a kick-starting boost into the next best version of you and beyond.

By definition (in short), stress is our body's **reaction to a trigger**; **a response** to a threat in any given situation. Anxiety (*according to* *the American Psychological Association*) is **an emotion characterized by feelings of tension, worried thoughts**, and physical changes like increased blood pressure (*apa.org*). It is also considered a sustained mental health ~~disorder~~ 'takeover' that can be triggered *by* stress, causing significant impairment in important areas of functioning. Wowzer. Tons of gray area in these definitions, but as a wise man once said "gray area is simply made up of black and white". Let's lean into this a bit…

A brilliant friend of mine (see chapter titled ***How To Change Your Group Of Friends***) by the name of Charlie Rocket, once said something along the lines of "Santa doesn't deliver presents in daylight. He delivers them at night when no one is up or around. Make sure you're looking around for your gifts when it's dark out." Pure gold. The message behind that is pure gold. We're going to dig up every gift that lies within these dark feelings. Our presents are lying around somewhere in our darkness. I hope the following words can serve as a flashlight.

If stress is a **reaction to a trigger**, and anxiety is an emotion characterized by **feelings of tension and worried thoughts**, then evidently **SOMETHING must trigger you in order for you to be stressed**, and there is **SOMETHING you must be worried about in order to evoke anxiety**. [*Read that back once more.*] What is the 'something' in your life? Don't answer that just yet. Stick with me here and let's break that question down even further.

Another brilliant friend of mine by the name of Srikumar Rao has this to say about stress (paraphrased): "**Stress, in some way, shape, or form, is a result of our seeking to control something in or around our lives**." His studies on stress have led him to the realization that in most cases, there is something in or around our lives that we would like to be a certain way, or we have an idea of how things SHOULD be, and because they are not – we stress. From this, I ask you: **what is it, in or around your current reality that you wish was different**? Wishing something was different is a form of seeking to control. Think about this for a minute.

We tend to blame our jobs, family, significant others, finances, debt-collectors, health, past, failures, and more for our stress; when in all actuality, **we're stressed because (in some way, shape, or form) those people and things are just not how we want them to be, and we wish to change that**. Belief that something or someone in your life is causing your stress won't ease your stress; that just gives you something to point your finger at – not empowering. It is not a person, place, or thing that is causing our stress; it is our seeking to control that person, place, or thing that is causing our stress. Learning and practicing the art of doing the **next best thing** is what **eliminates stress** in due time – empowering (see chapter titled *Mountains Are The Means. The Man Is The End. Mount Everest.*). Why stress about where you currently are, because you're not where you want to be...rather than focusing on being who you need to be, in order to get where you want to be? Why stress about a job, because it's not what you want to be doing...rather than focusing on who you need to be, in order to start doing what you want to be doing? I understand that taking the empowering route can be annoying, and more difficult; but this is the difference between sinking, and building a soul-powered ship that sails into a beautiful sunset. On a more serious note, this is the difference between stressing, and eliminating stress from your life – I say this, also from experience.

What we are bringing to light in this chapter is that stress, anxiety and depression (when really broken down) are not only evidence and proof that YOU WANT MORE AND BETTER FOR YOUR LIFE, BUT ALSO THAT YOU KNOW IT IS POSSIBLE/YOU ARE CAPABLE. You (most likely) don't stress about not being able to dunk a basketball. You don't stress about not being able to fly to the moon tonight. You don't get anxiety about gravity suddenly reversing itself and us falling into the sky. *[If you do, you're either an aspiring NBA player, Elon Musk, or...special.*] You DO stress over the possibility of failing. You DO get anxiety about things in your life going wrong. You DO get depressed about being stuck. Why? Because **you know** that there's a possibility that you might succeed, and you are capable of making it happen. **You believe** or have seen there is some way for things in your life to go right. **You feel** like you can do more. You are **anxious** about how much more you can accomplish. **When there is no possibility whatsoever for anything hopeful or better to occur, there is no stress, anxiety, or depression**. These dark emotions require a LIVING vessel. They need LIFE. When hope completely dies, there is nothing to be stressed about – numbness settles in, you don't feel, and emotions lie dormant.

Stress, anxiety, and depression are ultimately a means of your emotions communicating to you that you are in fact capable, and your body is preparing itself to go grow through what lies ahead. Do not confuse these with giving up. Your *presents* are somewhere around during these times, you just have to look within – it's dark out. Seek out people and things that spark your spiritual, emotional, and mental flashlights so that you may see clearer.

The American Psychiatric Association (*psychiatry.org*) states that depression is a "serious medical illness that negatively affects how you feel, the way you think and how you act...causes feelings of sadness...and can decrease a person's ability to function at work and at home." Let me ask you this question: **when the depth of your being knows that there is more within you, and more out of life that you are capable of tapping into...yet you're currently not – how else would you expect your body to respond?** Doesn't it make sense to naturally feel negative at a time like that? Wouldn't that affect your thinking? Wouldn't that dim your ability to perform at a high level? Especially over time?

These aren't bad things. Dark, yes. But dark is also when the stars come out. Dark is also when the Aurora (northern lights) come out to play. Dark is also when the moon can shine it's brightest. Dark is also when bioluminescent plankton (*google image this*) light up the ocean. Dark is when Santa delivers his presents. And most impressively, dark is the last thing we see before the sun rises. **WHAT ARE YOU GOING TO LOOK FOR IN YOUR DARKNESS?** Gifts & presents? Or wolves (stress)? Moonlight? Or predators (anxiety & depression)?

You will find whatever you look for. Some things might be harder to find than others, but by default of empowerment, the choice is still *yours*. The human body is a weird, interesting, complex thing. It sweats palms and armpits when we're nervous. It increases heart rate when we're running. It bumps up skin when we're cold. It raises hairs when we're stimulated. These are odd things, but nonetheless just things that our bodies do to prepare us for whatever it's ~~going~~ growing through. Your stress, anxiety, and depression come from the very same body that does all these other weird things. It's simply (and complexly) a means of preparing you for the unimaginable gifts you can find within your darkness. Don't be scared (or be scared if you want to). Just keep your eyes open.

Note

[*PTSD is a different ball game. I want to be clear in stating that everyone has different variations and degrees of stress; all to be taken very seriously. This chapter is by no means a one-size-fits-all guide nor solution. This chapter is simply meant to serve as a light for you to have more clarity in your darkness. The American Psychological Association defines Post Traumatic Stress Disorder as a "psychiatric disorder that can occur in people who have experienced or witnessed a traumatic event such as a natural disaster, serious accident, a terrorist attack, war/combat, rape or other violent personal assault...an estimated one in 11 people will be diagnosed PTSD in their lifetime. Women are twice as likely as men to have PTSD." (apa.org) Even in PTSD victims, the initial event lies outside of what the brain knows to be right/normal/ethical/discernable/digestible/controllable and more –*

and stress is triggered by the mental replaying of that initial event, due to the difficulty associated with recovering from it. PTSD in lots of cases leads to uncontrollable thoughts. However, PTSD has not conclusively been deemed insurmountable nor curable. There are many who have managed, even "mastered" the symptoms associated with PTSD. My hope is that the principles in this chapter & book will add to the list of methods. My love and upmost respect go out to any and all victims of PTSD, as well as their families.]

Please come back to this chapter and read it over and over again whenever these 'takeovers' consume you. You do not end here. You have an infinite amount of capability within you.

STRESS, ANXIETY, AND DEPRESSION ARE ULTIMATELY A MEANS OF YOUR EMOTIONS COMMUNICATING TO YOU, THAT YOU ARE IN FACT CAPABLE, AND YOUR BODY IS PREPARING ITSELF TO GROW THROUGH WHAT LIES AHEAD.

20

Your Life Is A Reflection/Byproduct Of Your Morning

I f you're still saying the words "I'm not a morning person", it's okay. We're going to save you in this chapter. Actually, the chapter on *affirmations* will save you. Please go read it. This chapter is here to solidify one simple truth: how you start your day has an impact on the outcome of your day. Hmm. It's almost too simple when its said like that. Here's how my friend Hal Elrod, author of *The Miracle Morning: The Not-So-Obvious Secret Guaranteed to Transform Your Life: Before 8am*, likes to say it: *"How you wake up each day and your morning routine (or lack thereof) dramatically affects your levels of success in every single area of your life. Focused, productive, successful mornings generate focused, productive, successful days—which inevitably create a successful life—in the same way that unfocused, unproductive, and mediocre mornings generate unfocused, unproductive, and mediocre days, and ultimately a mediocre quality of life. By simply changing the way you wake up in the morning, you can transform any area of your life, faster than you ever thought possible."* Everything that I have learned about the power of mornings comes from Hal's book and my experience from applying the principles within it. If you think that simply changing the way you go about your mornings won't change your life, please continue reading.

To start this off, allow me to share with you what I have been doing with my mornings for the past 2 years. Let's do some quick math. I wake up at 3:30am every day (for the most part). My workday currently doesn't begin until 7:30am. That's 4 hours from the time that I get out of bed to when the world requires that I do whatever it is that us humans do. There are 24 hours in a day. 7 days a week. Each morning my first 4 hours are spent doing focused, productive, successful things (I'll explain). 4 hours x 7 days = 28 hours (**or 1 day + 4 hours**) over the course of a week. So, by waking up at 3:30am each day, I've actually been able to create 1 additional day each week. That's 8 days in my week. While everyone else still thinks there's only 7. If I sound crazy right now, good. Bare with me. I am not saying you need to do this same thing. What I am sharing is simply ONE of the benefits I have reaped from prioritizing my mornings. Before we get into what to actually do with your mornings, let's lean into *why* this is so important. I'll answer 2 questions: Why is waking up early so important? And why is what you do first thing in your day so important?

Why is waking up early so important? Because YOU are important. From the moment that we wake up... life, family, friends, school, work, or some other thing is going to require your time, effort, and energy. Waking up early allows you the opportunity to FIRST spend your time, effort, and energy on YOU...BEFORE any thing or anyone else. If we do not create this time for ourselves, life will most certainly keep us busy enough with other things to ensure that we don't get a chance to. Living a life where you consistently wake up and immediately grab your phone to reply to messages/emails/calls, open up social media apps to scroll through entertainment and other people's lives, or handle work/school-related tasks IS NOT going to shape the life that you want; nor is it making productive time for your**self** FIRST. It's definitely not going to ensure you have a successful and fulfilled day – and this is why WHAT YOU DO FIRST THING in your day is so important.

Too many people, myself included, often underestimate the power of momentum. It does not only apply to good. You can have a 'hot streak' of bad as well, otherwise known as a slump. Once the wheels get turning in either direction, they become that much more difficult to stop – that is momentum. **You have got to ask yourself which direction your morning routine is pushing your momentum**. Take a second to think back on the last time you woke up late for something, and what kind of momentum that gave your day. It becomes ever more clear why one of the most common military practices is making the bed immediately after waking up. This gets the wheels turning in a way that encourages organization, discipline, neatness, self-control, patience, cleanliness, and a subtle reminder that **most things in chaos can be fixed with our actions**. That is the kind of momentum being carried into the rest of the day by those who make their beds immediately after waking up. This small practice gives **just one day** productive momentum; imagine the effect it has on a life built around days that begin this way.

Take a minute to also imagine the effect your current morning routine is having on your life. **Your morning is simply a momentum starter. Whichever direction you set foot on, be it positive or negative, will easily roll into the next part of your day.** Are you waking up and immediately scrolling social media? Are you waking up and immediately on your phone reading notifications? Are you waking up and immediately focusing your attention on something that doesn't serve you in a positive way?

Let me be the first to say that the state of your mental health is greatly impacted by how you begin your day. Our minds, bodies, and souls crave our attention. They deserve as much energy and focus as we give everything else in our lives. When neglected, we burn out, feel unfulfilled, and grow colorless. Your morning routine is the starting point not only for the life you wish to create, but also for the version of you required to manifest that very life you wish for. Putting yourself first each morning results in greater fulfillment. Too many of us are going through our days, coming home, and wrapping up, having done nothing for our SELF at any point. The morning, before anyone or anything else has a say in your day, is the best time to do YOU. Is waking up super early in the morning fun? Not exactly; but the practices I am about to share with you do turn into a form of self-love, and eventually habits. Falling in love with yourself goes far beyond any fun you can imagine; and when loving yourself becomes your habitual default...let's just say it's lit. So let's lean into what this looks like...

I first came across "Life S.A.V.E.R.S." in Hal Elrod's *The Miracle Morning*. I knew of things like meditation, journaling, etc. but Hal put what an ideal morning should look like into such a cool acronym that I just had to share it here:

S – silence (meditation)

A – affirmations (intentional talk with myself)

V – visualization (imagination to the max)

E – exercise (gym)

R – reading (book/podcast)

S – scribing (journaling)

I immediately implemented any of the above that were missing from my morning routine after completing *The Miracle Morning*. In the parenthesis next to each are my personal translations. It was made clear that these did not have to be done in any particular order, and I want to emphasize the same to you. I'll go even farther to say that you don't have to do these exact things, rather, tap into the benefits of each in whatever way that means for you. Each one of the "S.A.V.E.R.S." are extremely important to me because of the time with self that is required, so my ideal morning includes all of them, but even on mornings when

I do just one, the difference in my day is very noticeable.

It probably goes without saying...the benefits that I've seen and the life I've begun to reap by spending 28 hours per week meditating, intentionally speaking positively to myself, visualizing the life I wish to create for myself, exercising at the gym or doing yoga at home, reading books that have taught me the principles shared in this one, and journaling my thoughts down on paper. It's insanely life-redefining, and the best part is that all of this is done prior to my day starting, free of interruption. The growth, in many ways, is immeasurable.

What you do first thing with your mornings should, in sum, be things that fuel the inner most parts of who you are at your core. The important things (see chapter titled **Urgent vs. Important**). Things that – even if the entirety of your day was filled with uncontrollable events that made it suck – still keep you fulfilled, inspired, growing, and joyful. When your mornings are spent doing your **important** things, you *show up different*. You show up in mental place that allows you to tackle obstacles with greater ease. You show up in a spiritual place that allows you to better navigate through the different types of energies you might encounter. You show up in an emotional place that allows for you to maintain level-headedness through the highs and lows, and not want to punch everyone who annoys you. When you do not prioritize your mornings and the important things to do with them, you show up more susceptible to things that knock on the door of your lower vibrations – it's also just not as exciting. More often than not, I can tell how someone spent their morning by how they react to things during the day. You'll start to pick up on it as well.

This ultimately comes down to dedicating time to yourself BEFORE giving it away to your day and all that is required of you. There are people literally waking up every single day and immediately just...going. Going into their day. Affecting the energies of others before properly addressing their own. Reacting to everyone and everything. Seemingly not at all in control of their being. Don't be that person. Wake up. DO YOU. Do the day. Rinse. Repeat. IN THAT ORDER. Your life will either be a reflection of your putting yourself first each and every day, or a reflection of you going into your days without first taking care of yourself. The life you want is on the other side of you getting up early. Are you still not a morning person?

My morning routine

- 3:30am – Wake up, brush my teeth, put on gym clothes
- 3:40am – Yoga & stretching (with Adriene on YouTube)
- 4:10am – Meditation & Prayer
- 4:30am – Journal & visualization
- 4:55am – Leave for gym
- 6:30am – Coffee & walk with my queen
- 7:00am – Read or listen to a podcast

WHY IS WAKING UP EARLY SO IMPORTANT? BECAUSE YOU ARE IMPORTANT. FROM THE MOMENT THAT WE WAKE UP... LIFE, FAMILY, FRIENDS, SCHOOL, WORK, OR SOME OTHER THING IS GOING TO REQUIRE YOUR TIME, EFFORT, AND ENERGY. WAKING UP EARLY ALLOWS YOU THE OPPORTUNITY TO FIRST SPEND YOUR TIME, EFFORT, AND ENERGY ON YOU...BEFORE ANY THING OR ANYONE ELSE.

21

Mountains Are The Means. The Man Is The End. Mount Everest.

"Mountains are the means, the man is the end. The goal is not to reach the top of the mountains, but to improve the man." – Aron Ralston [*There's a good chance that you don't know who Aron Ralston is. That's not important. What is important is what he's done. It's simply incredible.*]

A movie titled *"127 Hours"* tells the story of Aron Ralston, and how he had to literally cut his arm off in order to survive. And I mean literally. With his own knife. Aron hiked a trail in the canyons that he'd hiked many times before, but on this particular day, crossed paths with a huge rock that unexpectedly moved and fell to a stopping point that his arm was caught between. It was there that Aron remained for 127 hours (about 5 days), hanging from this rock which jammed his arm between canyon walls. Had he chosen to stay in that place, his body would have rotted while he starved to death. He ultimately decided that if he was going to move on, there was a part of him that he would have to leave behind – that ended up being his arm. Today, he is the father of two little ones, and still remains an active hiker. Remember earlier in the book when we talked about how stepping into the next best version of you might require pieces of the current version of you to be left behind? Told you so.

But this quote though. The one at the beginning of this chapter. It's pure gold. Let's tap into it… A wise man once politely clowned the hype around Mount Everest. He found it humorous that so many people wanted so bad to reach the top of this mountain, yet so few realized and understood that one can only spend about 5 minutes up there. The weather is simply too inclement and unpredictable – it can be sunny with clear skies one minute, and viciously blizzarding the next. Most people still have this infatuation with the summit. Why though? The 'high' doesn't even last long.

Your 'summit' might be a bit different from that of a mountain. Maybe your summit is a financial goal. Maybe it's a career position, a different living location/condition, a placement, an award, a house, or some other reality that you have painted in your mind. Whatever it is – what happens when you acquire it/achieve it? Then what? Once a *fixed* goal is attained, you no longer have to chase it, and work is required to keep it. The issue is that we focus on our summits as if they are stopping points, or places where we can rest and then everything gets easier or better. We drive ourselves nuts in pursuit of reaching whatever it is that we're after, and the longer it takes, or the more resistance we face, the more of a negative light we place on our journeys there. We completely miss the point. WHICH IS WHY Aron Ralston states "The mountains (summits/things we're after) are the **means**, the man (you) is the **end**…" Once you set the goal (know what you want), great. Now it's about taking the steps that are going to get you there, and more importantly, **the person you become** while taking those steps. Focusing on the goal does not keep the mind stimulated in face of adversity – constantly becoming the person required to execute the next step does. **So your focus is better suited on the improvements you are making within yourself during your journey to the goal**. FOCUS has been said to stand for 'Follow One Course Until Successful.'

That is not the same as follow one *goal* until successful. **Course** implies a journey to where you're headed.

- Follow
- **O**ne
- **C**ourse
- **U**ntil
- **S**uccessful

The TRUE goal should be to improve yourself. On your way to wherever it is you want to be, or whatever it is you want to accomplish, you do not have control over what life is going to throw at you. This is precisely what happens on Mount Everest every single day – unpredictable weather. So what do Mount Everest guides do? They focus on getting climbers to what are known as base camps on the mountain. These are simply the **next best step** on the way up. Not only does altitude change as you climb, but so does temperature & weather. Rather than focusing on the top of the mountain, the goal is to acclimate the bodies of climbers to the rapid-changing conditions along the way. **Are your mind, body, heart, and soul conditioned for the summit you're pursuing? Life typically does not allow you to skip this part and go straight to your summit**. If Mount Everest Sherpas (tour-guides) took climbers directly to the summit without first acclimating their bodies, climbers would die. That's morbid. But in life, an example that perfectly conveys what this looks like is a person winning the lottery, or an athlete signing a major contract and then going bankrupt within months or a few years. Their mind, body, heart, and soul are simply not conditioned to handle millions of dollars.

A lot of us make the mistake of thinking that the mountain is the end, leaning into a thought pattern that is disempowering. If you don't climb the mountain, you've failed - and we build our identities on such things. **Should there be anything in this life that you wish to attain or become, it is simply a MEANS of either bettering or worsening you. This is why the goal is best suited as being a better version who you are.** By focusing on the improvement of yourself (rather than what you're pursuing), you set the parameters and criteria for ANYTHING that you pursue; you also operate from an empowering place because you're set on taking the **next best step** and highly effective actions to better you, rather than looking at how far you are from what you're pursuing.

Isn't it incredible how one of life's largest mountains has a way of showing us this lesson? I mean sure, everyone wants to reach the top of Everest. But no one talks about the person who you become on the way up the base camps. You're acclimating, you're becoming stronger, you're training your being to handle conditions you once were not built for, you're expanding what you once knew as limits, you're going beyond what you previously knew to be possible about yourself, you're breaking out of the shell of the old you.

"THE GOAL IS NOT TO REACH THE TOP OF THE MOUNTAIN, BUT TO IMPROVE THE MAN." IF YOU HAVE NOT YET REACHED WHAT YOU ARE AIMING FOR, DO NOT PANIC. YOU ARE ACCLIMATING. YOU ARE BECOMING STRONGER. YOU ARE TRAINING YOUR BEING TO HANDLE THINGS YOU ONCE WERE NOT ABLE TO. YOU ARE EXPANDING WHAT YOU ONCE KNEW AS YOUR LIMITS. YOU ARE GOING BEYOND WHAT YOU PREVIOUSLY KNEW TO BE POSSIBLE ABOUT YOURSELF. YOU ARE BREAKING OUT OF THE SHELL OF THE OLD YOU. DO NOT MISS OUT ON/TAKE FOR GRANTED THE IMPROVEMENTS YOU ARE MAKING, DUE TO BEING BLINDED BY WHAT YOU ARE PURSUING. CHANGE THE PURSUIT TO A BETTER YOU.

You may have to go back to your base camps (next best steps) at times, due to unforeseen things that life throws at you – that is not defeat.

It is only defeat if your only goal is to reach the top of the mountain. **Each time that you take the next best step in front of you, you are improving within. THAT is the goal**. When anyone asks you why you haven't made it to your 'summit', or judges you for how far you are from it, that is just proof of their outdated belief that reaching the top of the mountain is the goal. "The goal is **not** to reach the top of the mountain, but to improve the man." Remember this. Judge yourself by the improvements that you make within, not by how high you climb. Climb as high as you'd like but maintain the understanding that **you're climbing for the person you're becoming along the way – not to say you reached the highest point**. The goal is not to reach the top of the mountain. The mountain is simply the means. The goal is to improve you.

CLIMB AS HIGH AS YOU'D LIKE BUT MAINTAIN THE UNDERSTANDING THAT YOU'RE CLIMBING FOR THE PERSON YOU'RE BECOMING ALONG THE WAY – NOT TO SAY YOU REACHED THE HIGHEST POINT.

22

Time Is Not Something You 'Have'. It Is Strategically, Methodically, and Intentionally Made, Set Aside, or Created. Periodt.

Yes, the title of this chapter is lengthy, and no, that wasn't a typo. Periodt. I wanted to occasionally throw in subtle reminders that you can play by your own rules and do whatever you want in this lifetime - let the title of this chapter serve as one. I'm also going to end this paragraph here and move on to the next, which very well may disqualify this one as an official paragraph.

Basically what I'm getting at is that my middle school English teacher would probably get a headache from proofreading this, and more importantly, CREATE WHAT YOU WANT IN THIS LIFE BECAUSE EVERYTHING AROUND YOU HAS BEEN MADE UP OR CREATED BY SOMEONE ELSE - even time, or at least how we measure it today. The measurement of time began with sundials, and those just kept track of the period of daylight. Fast forward and here we are present day with years, months, weeks, days, hours, minutes, and seconds to keep track of what we know as *time*. Keep in mind that even the word 'time' was made up by someone at some point. The main purpose of this chapter is to bring 2 things to light:

1. You're not up against time.
2. No one just 'has' time - so stop saying you *wish you had more*...you do.

Let's address the former. You can only be up against time if you choose to be. By nature, time is actually gifted to us from the moment we become a life form. This moment is the first implication that *time* is WITH and FOR us. It's important to note that if you're reading this, approximately 200 million other would-be life forms were denied the gift of time in the same moment that you received it. Even more, if you're reading this, you still possess that gift - everyone breathing does.

Somewhere along the lines, we went from being blessed with this gift, to *"you better figure things out"* before *x,y, and z*. Not only is this narrative false, it's also backed by our perception of a word & method of measurement **made up** by someone else. Going off of the pure chances that we even become human, it would not seem crazy to believe that **we are actually in harmony with time**. Our lives, at some point having an end, is not so much indicative of time being against us, but rather gifted to us, to do something with during this window. What that 'something' might be is completely unique to you, the same way it is unique to everyone and everything else. Whatever that 'something' might be has no perception of time, or, at least not the same way we do. **Your impact, effect, or contribution is not bound to a specific amount of years, months, nor whatever else**. This is precisely why we are able to feel someone's impact, effect, or contribution before and after they are with us in physical form. It's also why you can meet someone and feel as though you've known them for years.

Breathe. Take in this moment. Don't get caught up in the clocks on the wall. And realize that there is no rush. You are precisely where you are in this moment, not just for a reason, but for a reason not bound by our perception of time. Your impact, effect, and contribution are harmonious with the NOW. It is happening as you breathe your next breath. Emphasize this.

As for the past, all you need to know are 3 things:

1. **Learn from it (don't act from a state of it).**
2. **It happened FOR you (not to you).**
3. **Every single moment/choice of it led you to exactly to where you are right now.**

As for the present:

- **It is harmonious with you as as an energy, being the only thing capable of simultaneously creating both the past and the future.**
- **Put yourself in a position to make your best choices.**

And as for the future, there are very few guarantees, those being:

- **It is a reflection of your present choices.**
- **The unexpected & uncontrollable will occur (so count on it).**

The sum of these truths equate to a greater one: **your being alive in the physical realm ultimately affirms that you are gifted with a *present* opportunity to impact, effect, and contribute beyond what we know as 'time'. What you choose to do with that opportunity is called life. Considering this truth, it would be foolish to believe that time is against us. Time and us are one,**

working within the same window of opportunity - the *present*.

Time may seem finite for us because our lives have an end (at least in the physical realm). But in the present, time is infinite. In the now, time hasn't happened yet, it is happening. And that *happening* is ongoing. What are you doing presently? Even more, what impact, effect, or contribution are you making presently? When your alarm goes off tomorrow morning, it will be at a present time that has an effect on an even later present time; in which you can either find yourself saying "I wish I had more time to do [x,y,z]" or "I am doing [x,y,z]". Time, as we know it, is not something that one just 'has', it is something you DO SOMETHING WITH. Some set theirs aside and create more, some spend theirs sleeping in and wishing they had more, some intentionally use theirs to take steps toward being the kind of person who acquires what they desire and creates the life they want, and others use theirs speaking of the reasons why they are not the kind of person who has what they want. **Who will you be?**

You have a gift within you - RIGHT NOW. *RIGHT NOW* has an impact, effect, and contribution to every moment that follows. *RIGHT NOW* has an impact, effect, and contribution to YOU - whether it be positive or negative. Life is simply made up of an infinite roll of **RIGHT NOW**. **Use this gift** to explore your infinite capabilities, so that you may be able to impact, effect, and contribute in your best & unique way - beyond what we know as "time".

TIME, AS WE KNOW IT, IS NOT SOMETHING THAT ONE JUST 'HAS', IT IS SOMETHING YOU DO SOMETHING WITH. SOME SET THEIRS ASIDE AND CREATE MORE, SOME SPEND THEIRS SLEEPING IN AND WISHING THEY HAD MORE, SOME INTENTIONALLY USE THEIRS TO TAKE STEPS TOWARD BEING THE KIND OF PERSON WHO ACQUIRES WHAT THEY DESIRE AND CREATES THE LIFE THEY WANT, AND OTHERS USE THEIRS SPEAKING OF THE REASONS WHY THEY ARE NOT THE KIND OF PERSON WHO HAS WHAT THEY WANT. WHO WILL YOU BE?

23

Let's Get Spiritual Without Getting Religious

Note: *I have an enormous amount of respect for all religions, which is why this chapter will lean into the core principles of religion, rather than acknowledging one while disregarding the others. The following words are also nothing more than my perspective.*

Can we all please stop pretending as though there isn't something much greater than us at work here? I mean, really. There is far too much happening all around and within us to not acknowledge that we are small, a spec in existence, and being looked out for by someone or something. Waterfalls, shooting stars, formations of stars, the oceans' boundaries, gravity, love, the human brain, the human body, the sun's perfect enough distance from the earth to not toast us, the architecture of a flower, the jobs of plants & trees, tornadoes, earthquakes, nature, daylight to nightfall, food growing from the planet, and the science that explains it all...DON'T JUST HAPPEN.

I was raised a Christian, and as I've grown older and expanded my consciousness, I've separated from the *titles* of religions and drawn closer to the *principles & beliefs that breathe life into them.* The idea that there is something greater than us at work in the universe, that is deserving of our gratitude and acknowledgement, in addition to our efforts to be a reflection of the highest forms of good that we are undoubtedly beneficiaries of - is something I can get behind. When we pull back the layers, added fluff, titles, names, of this energy most commonly known as God(s)...we are left with 1 common idea: **our existence is an opportunity, and more so a byproduct of *something* that is, at the least, deserving of our acknowledgement and gratitude; and in return for this opportunity, it doesn't seem insane to do the best that we can and be the best we can.**

What someone chooses to believe is completely up to them; that comes as one of the freedoms of being human. But is it so crazy to be thankful for the fact that you're breathing right now? Or just to be thankful, period? The *who* we should be grateful for is not as important as the principle behind being grateful. There is proof in this because whatever or whoever is keeping this whole shabang going, has not once stopped the show and asked for an applause, credit, nor acknowledgement. As a matter of fact, with or without our belief - the show goes on. We exist, we live, we die, and then who knows what. But...before we die (physically), why not explore if there's a "why" to our existence and try to grow more connected to the source of our being and all that we know?

I'm personally at a place in life where I believe in God, yes, but I don't know for certain if [*his/her/it's*] name is actually "God" or if that's just a name that some human made up thousands of years ago. In my acknowledgement of God, I also would hate to **not** acknowledge others (if there are). Like, what if God has a team of other Gods, and they all collectively work together to provide what we know as life, death, the universe and more - and I'm just sitting here only acknowledging one? [*So much unknown and gray area there, so I decided to start paying attention to the black and white that make up that gray area.*]

What I do believe, for certain, is that there is a reason for the way things are, there is a reason for my existence, yours, and everyone else's. I believe we are being cared for. I believe there is something special and unique about each of us, and due to the fact that we coexist, there is clearly much opportunity to contribute to one another, and so we should. I believe that something is responsible for a star, over 1 million times larger than earth, providing light to our planet every single day. I believe, at the least, that "God" is a possibility.

[*Speaking of possibilities, I also acknowledge that my beliefs may be totally incorrect and inaccurate! Maybe things are just happening. Maybe we do just exist and nothing more. Maybe there is no reason or purpose for things. Maybe everything that we experience in life ends with science and there is nothing beyond that. However, I also acknowledge that this is undoubtedly the most colorless paragraph of this book. To remove hope, yearning for understanding & purpose, reason, and connection, is to remove the quintessence of our existence as humans.*]

I was taught that God is omnipresent, that he, his son (Jesus), and the holy spirit are one, that God is love, that God has given us the freedom of choice, and ultimately that my acceptance of God would mean that he dwells within me. **What I have been willing to let go of are names and titles, because I don't believe they hold as much value as what they represent and the energy they carry.** When I extract ONLY the principles, I am left with a beautiful and infinite realization: **My acceptance of there being something bigger than me, allows for my submission and exploration of a purpose for me and beyond me. My understanding that I have been gifted with the ultimate power of choice allows for:**

- my deciding to do *good or bad*
- my indulging in the highest or lowest vibrations
- my choosing right or wrong
- my understanding that every single person has this same

exact freedom of choice.

Also, that if <u>the highest form of energy and the creator of all</u> <u>things</u> be omnipresent, be love, be harmonious - then I too am love, I too am harmonious with all things that make up this one energy, and I too am an extension of this energy and creator. Finally, that if omnipresent means everywhere, then this <u>energy/being/spirit</u> is not only IN me, but is also in everything and everyone else, and has been in every single second, moment, and experience of my life - even in my being molested as a child, even in the death of loved ones, and even in the darkest and most painful of times of human existence. If these things be true, it also is true that I am God, You are God, We are an extension of God, and we therefore possess the infinite power that God be - to the extent of God's will, which is in alignment with our own will and our own choices. (Please feel free to replace the name "God" with what/who you believe in.)

Connection is far too misunderstood and unintentionally overlooked in our quest for more out of this life. When you find yourself longing for more of you, more of life, deeper spirituality, deeper love...be still and look around you. You will find that we are one and the same as all things created by the hands of a higher power that YOU HAVE ACCESS TO. Every flower, leaf of a tree, blow of the wind, cloud, color and more, come from the same source that we do. Everything that exist is a harmonious extension of the energy that created us - therefore, you are capable of creating just as much beauty and astonishment as the source that created you. And if that source be omnipresent, then it is also within you. Everything is one. We just have to allow our mind, body, and soul to see that.

OUR EXISTENCE IS AN
OPPORTUNITY, AND
MORE SO A BYPRODUCT
OF SOMETHING THAT
IS, AT THE LEAST,
DESERVING OF OUR
ACKNOWLEDGEMENT
AND GRATITUDE; AND IN
RETURN FOR THIS
OPPORTUNITY, IT
DOESN'T SEEM INSANE
TO DO THE BEST THAT
WE CAN AND BE THE
BEST WE CAN.

24

The Universe Is On Your Side. I'll Prove It.

J ust realized I put myself in a bit of a pickle by saying I'll prove it - but here goes nothing! The best way to get this point through is stories and examples, so let's start with one of my favorites about a man named Jørn Utzon. You've ~~probably~~ definitely never heard of this man. But I bet you've heard of the Sydney Opera House... He's the architect. Yup, the original designer. El jefe. The guy who conceptualized the thing. Plot twist: he never got to step foot inside, let alone see the thing. The man was not invited to it's opening!

Photo Credit: www.sydneyoperahouse.com

Being that this building went up in 1973, there's plenty of room for miscommunication and inaccuracy in how this story is told over the years, so I'll do my best to tell you everything that went wrong during its construction. (Look at the photo above and the legacy Jørn left behind to see *what went right*) Let's start with the unpopular opinion that Jørn was not easy to work with, especially for others in his field. One of his idols, Erik Gunnar Asplund, had a way of getting what he wanted (financially) by means of resigning from projects in the middle of their progress. Jørn followed those footsteps, maybe a little too closely, and ultimately ended up walking away from the Sydney Opera House on his own will. I'm not here to discuss whether this was justified or not, but I will tell you that at the time of his resignation in March of 1966, Jørn was owed $100,000 in fees. He threatened to quit, believing the government would back down and pay him, but they did not end up doing so. After the meeting where he was denied his pay, Jørn ended up walking behind the building where he was, and climbing a wall that was accompanied by a 21-ft drop, just to avoid the embarrassment of being denied in front of the press. [Lets take a second here to think about how embarrassed you would have to be to willingly take on a 21-foot drop instead of the front door.] About a month later, Jørn and his family traveled to Hawaii under false names, again in an attempt to avoid the press.

We should also take note of the beauty and timelessness of the Opera House, which is arguably ahead of it's time even today; imagine the resistance Jørn must have faced 70 years ago while trying to sell others on his design! Time and time again, throughout the development of this project, Jørn was faced with opposition in the form of personal agendas, lack of budget due to personal agendas, dislike of his character, the diagram of his design being found in a rejection pile, delays, being questioned on every single decision made, being questioned on schedule, being questioned on costs, and furthermore, his name not even being mentioned at the opening ceremony. He was also banned from the Danish Architects Association, threatened with a huge tax bill if he resumed his Danish citizenship, and basically spent the rest of his days in exile. This particular story doesn't have a blatant happy ending. This happy ending comes in the form of something extremely subtle, silent, and free of desire for recognition - The Sydney Opera House.

The next story is that of Nikola Tesla. Where most see one of the most tragic stories of all time, I see one of the most compellingly beautiful. Today his last name is more popular than he himself was, but lets bring light to what his experience of life was like during his time here. A lot would argue that Nikola was the greatest scientific genius of all time, yet the things he went through seemingly did not reflect that. As an immigrant from Serbia, Nikola faced a great deal of poverty, slander, unfair & unequal treatment, and plenty of being ignored and overlooked. This dude came into the States, containing one of the brightest minds ever known to man, and due to a lack of funds and not writing things down, went practically unnoticed. When he first arrived, he sought out the great Thomas Edison and ended up working under him for a while - and for almost nothing.

During this time, not only did Nikola far exceed what was required of him at Edison's company, he also brought a handful of ideas that were so far beyond the comprehension of one of the greatest inventors of all time (Thomas Edison) that he was constantly rejected the opportunity to work on them! What you might find most bizarre is that Edison purposely gave Nikola an almost impossible task, and promised $50,000 would lie on the other side of it. Nikola performed that task with ease, made Edison richer because of it, and when he finally asked for the $50,000 - Edison responded by saying he was joking when he made that offer. I know what you're thinking…the disrespect is real. It actually gets worse.

Nikola of course left Thomas Edison and went on to do his own thing…But with about $0. After coming up with one of the greatest electrical inventions of all time, he sold his patent for cash and royalties in order to stay afloat. Nikola later ended up destroying the contract that upheld his royalty payments, out of pure kindness of heart, in order to help save the company & person that purchased his patent. That company, known today as Westinghouse, went on to make millions while Nikola received none. In sum, Nikola ended up walking away from what would have been billions of dollars, ultimately because he was kind. He later died with a tremendous amount of debt, but to many, is known as one of the *would-be* wealthiest people to ever walk the planet. This story also has a subtle, happy ending - the spark of an incredible leader by the name of Elon Musk, who today runs a company known as Tesla - one of the most thought-leading companies in it's space.

You are probably catching wind of where this chapter is headed by now, but I've got one more story for ya. This one of a boy who had to experience the downside of every topic written in this book, in order to later become the author of it. Let's start with being born into a world where both parents weren't together. Having a mom sound enough to quit her addictions to drugs because of me. Hopping from shelter to shelter with that single mother. Abusive day cares while she worked to provide a life for me. A father who was most definitely there, but not as present as the best of us would have liked. Court-ordered weekend visitation rights with that father. Eviction after eviction with that mother. School hopping due to the frequent moving with that mother. Sexual and psychological abuse on the weekends when I was supposed to be with that father. Taking those learned behaviors as a child and being unaware enough to project them onto people I deeply cared about. Living with that regret for decades. Going through teenage years and into adulthood without ever speaking of those times. An actual famine with that mother. Real poverty. Winters with no heat. Section 8 apartments with leaky ceilings. Neighborhoods with the kind of violence a child should never see. Traumatizing experiences. Plenty of being bullied. Nightly gunshots just footsteps away from my front doors that became the normal. Lots of hunger. Knowing every cause for that mother's tears. Plenty of not knowing what tomorrow would look like. Somehow making it to college. Pursuing a basketball dream. Somehow being forced to drop out of college. Living with that mother and her husband into my late 20s. Working 2-3 jobs at a time over the course of years. Starting a music career. Eating every failure of that music career. Eventually moving out on my own. Restoring relationships of my past without the help of the people I thought would take the lead on doing so. Self-healing. Self-discovery. Learning to forgive. Forgiving myself. Learning to love. Learning to break generational and systemic poverty. Breaking myself. Piecing myself back together. And eventually combining the forces of everything mentioned above to cultivate and mold what you currently have in your hands.

The common theme here is that none of the people in any of these stories saw the imprint they would eventually leave behind. While these stories were happening, none of these people caught wind of what would become of them. There are billions of stories just like these, and yours is currently being written. Most of us can think back to an undesirable time that had zero signs of upside. A time where there really was no light at the end of the tunnel. I chose not to drop any cuss words in this book, so instead I'll say we've all been through some 'things'. In real time, it's extremely difficult to grasp the concept that life is happening FOR you. But don't be so selfish. Lock in on there being a future version of you. Keep that version of you in mind as you *grow* through your present experiences, whether fun or hellish.

The present is an opportunity for you to plant your seeds into this life, and you do not necessarily need desirable circumstances in order to do so. As a matter of fact, based on the overwhelming list of stories like the ones in this chapter, the less desirable your circumstances, the greater your impact can be when you choose to keep ~~going~~ growing. In the poopiest of times, you've got to know that you can simply be the kind of person required to overcome the challenges in front of you, and trust that your circumstances ARE favorable.

The universe is not out to get you, but to stretch you farther than you can currently imagine. When you fell while learning to ride a bike, the universe was not trying to hurt you, but rather show you that even pieces of your skin detaching from your body can't stop you. You can get right back up. Cry if needed. Recover from a broken bone. And become who you are today. Even more, you WILL leave *something* behind - make life about that something. Don't be so selfish. Life is constantly happening FOR you, not to you.

THE PRESENT IS AN OPPORTUNITY FOR YOU TO PLANT YOUR SEEDS INTO THIS LIFE, AND YOU DO NOT NECESSARILY NEED DESIRABLE CIRCUMSTANCES IN ORDER TO DO SO.

25

Consistency Is Not Key. It's The Door Between You and The Life You Want.

I'm going to be straightforward with you: you are not a 7, 10, nor 30 day challenge away from the life of your dreams. You are unique. You are infinite. You are complex. You are not bound by time. You are ongoing. The gurus who encourage challenges for a specific period of time are coming from a good place; they are trying to kick-start your potential. But quite frankly, if your mind is wrapping time around anything in regard to your improvement, you're being robbed of the magic behind true consistency, and potentially setting yourself up for a false summit. A 30 day challenge might be effective in kick-starting a behavior, but consistency lies far beyond the walls of that final day.

Consistency has no attachment to a final result, rather, it is a state of being. And it is from this state that you may manifest many different results - be it a six pack, reaching the top of a mountain, finishing school, securing the job you want, securing the bag you're after, achieving the goals you've set, gaining recognition, accomplishing great feats, winning, or anything else. These are all byproducts of BEING consistent. There is a very dangerous rumor going around that hints at consistency being something we can negotiate with. CONSISTENCY IS NON-NEGOTIABLE. You either are or you are not. It requires complete and total submission, and requires such because anything and everything that you want can be accessed through its power.

Yes, I'm totally saying that consistency is one of those spirits that requires your soul in exchange for whatever it is that you want out of life. Look, if you look around at your life, everything that you have has either come in the form of blessings or as a result of how consistent YOU have been in regard to showing up to manifest those things. (Note that manifestation, in this book, is simply a return on investment) So therefore, anything that you do not yet have, is a reflection of how consistent YOU have been in regard to showing up to manifest those things as well. **Inconsistencies in your life are mirrors to the consistency of your being**.

'Sticking with it' is persistence. BEING the kind of person who sticks with it is consistency. Consistency does not shift nor alter when faced with circumstance, no matter the magnitude of disruption. Again, this is a non-negotiable state of being. Make the choice right now as you read these words, that you hereby pronounce yourself a CONSISTENT BEING. THAT YOU FOLLOW THROUGH ON ANY THING YOU TOUCH IN THIS LIFETIME, AS A RESULT OF YOUR BEING CONSISTENT. **At the top of the mountain you are trying to reach, lie the continuation of the consistent being that you are. At the attainment of whatever you desire, lie the continuation of the consistent being that you are**. Your consistent *being* needs no attachment to an end result, no matter how beautiful or desirable that end result may be, because you are a perpetual energy capable of manifesting infinite possibilities. You are built to continue onward with all the good that you are, in the face of your achievements and greatest accomplishments, because they are simply a byproduct of your CONSISTENT BEING.

There is no off switch for your being. So decide today that moving forward your being will be **consistent** in all that you do, pursue, attain, think, speak, and more. **Nothing will call for the sacrifice of your consistency except for things that are disharmonious with the life you wish to create**. Therefore, be not afraid to be non-stop in the alignment of your highest self. Don't be scurrred (scared, for my less *hip* people) to commit to your best self - submit to it, so that your daily decisions reflect that commitment. Your daily decisions are a reflection of your commitment to yourself already (yup, right now). Meaning you can look at what you're currently doing, or not doing, on a day to day basis, and tell how committed to yourself you actually are.

Be committed to BEING CONSISTENT - which is a state of being. No past-tense there. You just are. Forever. Consistent. And allow this to be. Non. Freaking. Negotiable. When the old, not as lit, wants-to-do-something-stupid-to-compromise-what-you're-working-towards version of you tries to come out and play... Come back to this chapter for a reminder of who the (insert cuss word) you are.

CONSISTENCY HAS
NO ATTACHMENT TO
A FINAL RESULT,
RATHER, IT IS A
STATE OF BEING.
AND IT IS FROM
THIS STATE THAT
YOU MAY MANIFEST
MANY DIFFERENT
RESULTS

26

The Difference Between Happiness and Joy

One comes and goes with external circumstance, and the other is a state of being. Look, I understand that a great deal of the ideas within this book go against the common grain, but if you allow yourself to buy in and be accepting of these words, I promise the worst that will happen is your becoming **contagiously-gold** and **emotionally, mentally, and spiritually bulletproof**. Far too many of us are left susceptible and vulnerable to things and people outside of ourselves. One thing that should be unshakable is your *joy*.

Happiness is great! It really is. It paves the way for smiles, rolling on the floor in laughter, good times, enjoyment, good vibes, great memories, and more. But what happens to happiness when a loved one passes away? Or when we get fired from a job...or when plans get ruined...dreams get shattered...or a relationship ends badly...or we drop our ice cream on the ground...or we are doubting ourselves...or we don't have enough money to do the things we need to. What happens to happiness then? It is seemingly absent, and replaced with undesirable feelings. So at it's core, happiness is greatly dependent upon what is going on, in and around our lives. It can be snatched in an instant.

There should be at least one thing that is all YOURS to keep - free of any worry that it may be taken. At least one thing that stays in place, no matter what. A safe place for your dwelling, no matter what might be happening around you. A place within, where none of life's earthquakes (literal or emotional) can reach. Eternally accessible to you, but not to anything nor anyone else. You are deserving of such a thing. From this day forward, that is your *joy*.

Every word of this book is meticulously threaded together in order to lead to all-things-YOU. **Joyful**, in its simplest form means full of joy. *Full* describes the INSIDE of something. Thus implying that JOY is immaterial and it, by nature, is INTERNAL. If this be something that lies within us, it is no wonder why most never find it - it's much more popular to pursue happiness.

Happiness is found in things, moments, times, and places. *Joy* is found within, and therefore goes wherever you go, is experienced in everything you do, and can be felt at all times, regardless of circumstance. It does not belong to, nor does it have any attachment to anything or anyone except YOU. It needs nothing more than a vessel to fill. And this is the beauty of it...purely by your existence, and your existence alone...you are gifted with, entitled to, in harmony with, in ownership of, and in no danger of losing - *joy*.

Even in losing yourself, joy will remain with you until you find you again. This is what we call truly immovable. Not only should you seek it out, but furthermore, seek to experience life through its lens. If you are wondering how, you are in the right place. All it takes is a decision, and a reason. I have decided to experience life from a place of *joy* simply because I can; because of everything mentioned in this chapter, and because it's way more fulfilling than not doing so. I love having something that can not be robbed. I love feeling a sense of belonging in every thing I experience. I love being chill, and internally lit at all times for no specific reason. I love feeling loved and as though every single second of every single moment in every single day of every single week in every single month is conspiring FOR me. I love that in the midst of any sadness, hard time, death, loss, terrible experience, card declined, rejection, abuse, slump, and beat-down…I STILL HAVE THIS SOMETHING INSIDE OF ME THAT IS ETERNALLY ACHING OF THANKFULNESS, FULFILLMENT, LOVE, AND UTTER CONFIDENCE THAT I AM WHOLE AND ALIVE AND STILL BLESSED WITH THE OPPORTUNITY TO FEEL THE VERY THING I AM INSANELY MOTIVATED TO BE WRITING IN ALL CAPS RIGHT NOW… *JOY*.

It's time to grab hold of yours right now. Go grab a pen. Repeat the following aloud: MY JOY IS MINE. I'LL TAKE HAPPINESS AS IT COMES BUT MY BATTERIES RUN OFF OF THE ETERNAL STATE OF BEING THAT I NOW KNOW AS JOY. FROM THIS MOMENT FORWARD, I CHOOSE TO BE JOYFUL, AND FOREVER MORE EXPERIENCE LIFE FROM THE LENS OF MY JOY, SIMPLY BECAUSE I CAN, I AM ENTITLED TO IT, AND WELL, ITS UNSHAKABLY BUILT INTO MY DNA SO I MIGHT AS WELL ENJOY IT - PUN INTENDED. IN THE FACE OF ANY AND ALL EXTERNAL CIRCUMSTANCE & EXPERIENCE, NO MATTER HOW INCREDIBLE OR HEART-WRENCHING, I CHOOSE TO REMAIN JOYFUL FOR THE FOLLOWING REASON(S):

I have beautiful people in my life + so much love to give to those people

NO THING, NO BODY, NO MOMENT NOR EVENT CAN EVER TAKE THIS AWAY FROM ME. BECAUSE I AM JOY. AND *JOY* IS FOREVER ROOTED IN MY BEING.

Take a moment to close your eyes, and visualize placing your reason(s) into a lock-box, then opening your heart and placing that lock-box inside. Seal your heart and toss the key to that lock-box into the abyss.

AND THIS IS THE
BEAUTY OF IT...
PURELY BY YOUR
EXISTENCE, AND
YOUR EXISTENCE
ALONE...YOU ARE
GIFTED WITH,
ENTITLED TO, IN
HARMONY WITH, IN
OWNERSHIP OF, AND
IN NO DANGER OF
LOSING - JOY.

27

Call Your Mom/Dad. Pick Up When They Call.

To anyone reading this, who has experienced the loss (in the physical realm) of a parent, or maybe even both parents: I take this moment to send my deepest condolences, and also to let you know that you may rid yourself of any and all things aside from the <u>love</u> that was shared between you and your mother/father. That love is all that need remain - not regret of any sort.

It's much more imperative that you embrace the underlying principles of this chapter, rather than the title. There are two types of treatment towards parents that we are addressing - unaware and begrudging. Let's begin with the former. Due our being the child of our parents and *not* being the parent of our mother/father, we will never know exactly what it feels like to be them. Even in having your own child, your experience of parenting will be greatly different from theirs. Basically what I am saying is, YOU WILL NEVER KNOW WHAT IT FEELS LIKE TO HAVE BEEN PART OF WHAT IT TOOK TO BRING YOU INTO THIS WORLD. It is literally impossible to experience being the parent of yourself, which is why **you will never know what it feels like to love you the way they do**. With this in mind, it becomes easier to understand that you will also never quite grasp what it means to your mother/father when they hear your voice through the phone. It's extremely easy to be so disconnected from this fact, that not picking up a call or 2 seems harmless. When we get in the habit of this, or in the habit of not MAKING time to call them, we rob ourselves of an incredible blessing: the opportunity to make someone's day in a way that is incomprehensible to yourself.

One phone call can serve as a reminder that your mother/father have somewhat of an extension of themselves out here. It can touch a part of their minds and hearts in an incomparable way. Even if the conversation isn't the way you'd prefer it be. This isn't about you. You won't 'get it' because you aren't your parent! 'It' is a feeling, **unique to them**, in the connection between you two. LOVE is worth allowing them moment after moment of access to that feeling - and this is what the phone call is about. *Love.* Nothing else. Not that they're annoying to talk to. Not that they don't know how to stop talking. Not that there's nothing but drama when you do call. This is solely about **putting yourself in a position to be able to set yourself aside**, and allow your mother/father to just be who they are while you listen. We might even learn something.

We often forget that before we were born, our parents had their own lives, the same way we do now. They were a version of themselves that we will probably never get to know. Things mattered to them that we may never learn about. They have experiences and traumas that we typically never ask about. If you truly want to, there is an opportunity to expand the relationship between you and your mother/father beyond where it currently sits.

I, of course, acknowledge that there may be circumstances that make all of this less and less of a one-size-fits-all approach, but the truth remains that **there is no circumstance whatsoever that outweigh the love (no matter how seemingly present or absent) a parent**

has for their child. This is something we will never fully comprehend until we ourselves have children (I say this as someone who does not yet have any; but awareness & compassion have allowed me a great deal of insight in this regard). From a place of accountability & responsibility, *which are the underlying principles of this chapter*, there need be no circumstance whatsoever that we, as children of our parents, allow to outweigh that love.

"Outweigh" in this chapter means any of the following: cloud your judgement, operate from a place of toxicity, be vindictive and spiteful, or allowing disagreements/their wrongdoings and shortcomings to determine how you treat/respond to them. There is a way to separate your feelings from how you treat someone, and your parents are deserving of such a thing. Exercise that option because you are MORE SO deserving of not being slave to anger, grudges, lack of forgiveness, and disagreement. Those are some heavy weights to carry around through life, and if unaddressed, present the risk of manifesting themselves down the road, in very subtle and undesirable ways.

There are only 2 ways to shrink the magnitude of negative impact that a parent may have had on you. Only 2 ways that allow us to see exactly how small the problems we have in our relationship with our parents are. Only 2 ways to realize you may be taking your mother/father for granted. One being death. The other being your choice and decision to *LOVE* them **UNCONDITIONALLY TODAY, in the way THEY best receive love**, not just the best way you give. Start with a phone call.

THIS IS SOLELY ABOUT PUTTING YOURSELF IN A POSITION TO BE ABLE TO SET YOURSELF ASIDE, AND ALLOW YOUR MOTHER/FATHER TO JUST BE WHO THEY ARE WHILE YOU LISTEN. WE MIGHT EVEN LEARN SOMETHING.

28

What Happens When You Don't Write Things Down

Take a good look around you. No, really. Look at everything around you right now. Where are you sitting? At home? In your room? At work? In a cafe? In your car? Friend's house? Now shift your attention to the bigger picture of where you are. You're either in a building, an establishment of some sort, a vehicle, or something that was constructed by someone at some point (or maybe you're someone like me and you're hanging out in nature). What I'm getting at here is that if you think of HOW everything around you was built into existence, you will realize that almost all of it began as an idea, that was then made into a *blueprint*. This is the first step of any construction project, following the conception of it - getting it from out of mind, and on to paper. This VERY practical step has made way for the homes, buildings, highways and more that make up what we now call neighborhoods, cities, states, and countries. Why is it then, that people continue to have an IDEA of what they want their life to look like, yet not write it down?

We have literally built civilizations and life as we know it from blueprints. This gives me the idea that if I want to have an incredible

169

day, my first step, evidently, should be writing that out in as much detail as possible. At the least, it wouldn't be crazy of me to think so. What would be crazy however, is for me to have a brilliant & vivid picture of the life I want for myself...in my head...and to just keep it there...wanting it to become real life...rather than spend time daily, writing it out onto something tangible that I can see and hold IN REAL LIFE. It would be crazy because statistically speaking, things written down actualize more than things that do not. Let's delve into more of the why...

When we write things down, say in a journal session...what is going to come out onto paper are all the things that are currently top of mind; the things that have our attention. This is important because often times, due to overcrowding up there, we won't have clarity around our thoughts. So, writing things down shows us what's on our minds, and at the same time, frees up space for whatever might come next. *Clarity* is simply quality of sight & understanding. With experts estimating that we think anywhere from 60,000 to 80,000 thoughts per day...if you were to write down 0 of those thoughts...what do you think your mental clarity (quality of sight & understanding) would look like? Oh, and we haven't even mentioned the tasks that you're doing throughout the day. Ohhh, AND the people you're dealing with as well.

Building the life you want is a construction project, and you are constantly under construction; which means you should constantly be writing things down. What you write becomes like a daily progress report of the being that you are. You'll be able to SEE and process what you're feeling. You'll remember more! Because you're much more likely to remember something YOU generate yourself, than say, what you're reading right now (insert sad face). You will clear your mind and allow for higher thinking. Million-dollar ideas need room to be born! You will **feel** more productive even if you technically aren't! We tend to ACT how we FEEL!

When we don't write things down, we fog up our window of clarity. We carry excess weight. We store a lot of unnecessary information that comes out in the form of pimples on your face. [That was a joke with some truth to it.] We keep our ideas and desires suffocated, which eventually kills them. We end up unintentionally ignoring things that really need our attention & care. We stockpile junk, which attracts more junk. All of this manifests a repeat of the same - ultimately blocking the light that our minds are. **And with our minds holding a great deal of responsibility for the life we create, we end up limiting what is actually an infinite power, and creating a life that is LESS THAN the one we desire - all because the one we desire never got to see the light of day** (aka make it on paper).

Go get a *brand new* journal today (brand new makes us take it seriously). And commit to yourself right now, that you will do YOUR BEST to not let a day go by without scribbling down some words. Journals don't have to be this perfect thing that is done correctly. It's literally just a place to store your thoughts; you can make it more than that if you choose. For now, when you open that thing up, just start with WHATEVER COMES TO MIND. Even if it's *"...umm idk what to write right now. Tarik told me I should do this and so here I am. Birds. Clouds. Water bottles. Peeling my scab. Soap! Gotta go bye."* Yes, even this is fine.

There are no rules. Just please, do not NOT write things down. You did not come this far just to suffocate the life you're capable of creating. You are the kind of person who writes things down. You are the kind of person who writes things down. **You are the kind of person who writes things down**! *Soap!*

WHEN WE DON'T WRITE THINGS DOWN, WE FOG UP OUR WINDOW OF CLARITY. WE CARRY EXCESS WEIGHT. WE STORE A LOT OF UNNECESSARY INFORMATION THAT COMES OUT IN THE FORM OF PIMPLES ON YOUR FACE.

29

What Got You Here, Won't Get You There

S tarting this chapter off is challenging because it should be made clear that core, foundational principles can, and probably will, always be applicable in the face of almost any circumstance. So if a core principle of yours is *the belief that you can overcome any setback*, good; that is timeless. Now on the other hand, imagine you're carrying a 50 lb bag in your left hand, and you aren't allowed to set it down until you've walked 30 miles. At some point, your left arm is going to wear down, and it won't suffice to keep the bag in that hand. You'll switch to your right, maybe use both hands, or toss the bag up on one of your shoulders. Life requires a similar fashion of adaptation.

It's ironic how easily we'll switch up our positioning when we're carrying something that is too heavy, but how *resistant* we are to switching up our routines when our lives aren't where we want them to be. **You will wear yourself down by not being willing to change something within, while in pursuit of a more fulfilling life. The more willing you are to make drastic shifts within, the less resistance you will find yourself facing, and the stronger you will grow the newly exercised parts of your being.** *What got you here, won't get you there* means that you will have to shed some skin, break free from your cocoon, or leave pieces of you behind, in order to get to your next destination. The most successfully-fulfilled people I know in this life are the ones who willingly separate from pieces of themselves in order to step into a *more whole* version of themselves.

Turn off the back-up alarms. Close out the social media apps. Say no to sacrificing your time and productivity just to binge. Say yes to finding a group of friends who will elevate who you are. Go in the opposite behavioral & habitual direction that you've been going, if you are not manifesting the fulfillment you want. Make it overwhelmingly clear to yourself that WANTING SOMETHING DOES NOT MEAN YOU WILL GET IT. I can actually almost guarantee you that wanting something will not get you that *something*. Wanting to be a morning person, or wanting to have more time to read and do things that light you up is not enough to make those things actualize. **Life is a reflection of who you are, not what you want. LIFE IS A REFLECTION OF WHO YOU ARE, NOT WHAT YOU WANT**.

If you want a better job, YOU HAVE TO *BECOME* THE KIND OF PERSON WHO GETS A BETTER JOB. If you want more money, YOU HAVE TO *BECOME* THE KIND OF PERSON WHO ATTRACTS MORE MONEY. If you want better friendships, YOU HAVE TO *BECOME* A BETTER FRIEND AND THE KIND OF PERSON WHO ATTRACTS BETTER FRIENDS. If you want drama and toxicity removed from your life, YOU HAVE TO *BECOME* THE KIND OF PERSON WHO IS UNDISTURBED BY DRAMA AND FREE OF TOXICITY. Want it ≠ get it. **Want it + time invested in it + willingness to adapt to get it = get it.**

Whatever got you here, to this place of wanting more, will not get you *there*. What will get you there is being elastic, and willing to let go of what got you here, SO THAT **YOU MAY BECOME WHAT YOU ARE TRYING TO GET YOUR LIFE TO BE** - be it rich, wealthy, financially-free, fulfilled, enlightened, joyful, at peace, free of anxiety, yoda-like, more loving, etc. What ever you want out of life, you must first become at the core of your being. And if your life is "fine", I lovingly am here to tell you that you are capable of more if you want it. We all should be waking up in tears of joy for the overwhelming amount of abundant fulfillment we are experiencing. Until we get there, let's not be stubborn. Let's be willing to switch the 50 lb bag into whatever position we need, as many times as we need, in order to continue forward.

WHAT WILL GET YOU THERE IS BEING ELASTIC, AND WILLING TO LET GO OF WHAT GOT YOU HERE, SO THAT YOU MAY BECOME WHAT YOU ARE TRYING TO GET YOUR LIFE TO BE

30

Go Vegan. Not In An Intrusive Way. Here Is My Plea.

On behalf of anyone who has ever shoved veganism in your face, anyone who has ever judged you or considered you to be less of a human being for your eating choices, and on behalf of anyone who treated you as though you are wrong while obnoxiously communicating to you their views with complete disregard to your own – I am sorry. I am so incredibly sorry. Let it be known that this book is a safe space for you to be who you are, and ultimately a tool for your growth and personal expansion. This chapter is meant to begin a conversation within yourself, not tell you what to do. I am by no means a nutritionist nor dietitian, but I have studied food for the past 4 years of my life. Before going vegan 4 years ago, I pretty much ate what was familiar to me, and did so based on what was taught to me. In the following pages, I'll simply be sharing my perspective along with some of the things I've learned during this time, and from that, I hope for you to have new insight & perspective. If you would be kind enough to open your mind, I believe you will walk away with something special. I'll break this down into segments in order to help myself not go on a rant.

Why I went vegan

A few years back, I was going through one of the most transforma-
tional times of my life. It was mid 2016 and personal growth was brand
new to me. A whole new world, actually. The lack of movement and
change in my life bred a special kind of frustration within, leading to a
drastic willingness to suddenly flip my world upside down. I was so
sick of the repetitive experiences, same year after year nonsense, and
escapism that I was indulging in. It was the first time in my life that I
realized *wanting a different life meant switching everything.* I also realized
there was nothing about my current life (at the time) that I was SO
needing to hold on to, that I could not make some changes. My life was
dry and unfulfilled. Anything I was doing remained stagnant. I made a
decision: do one new thing every day for 100 days straight. Whether
it be listen to an album, watch a movie, take the train somewhere, fly
somewhere, write something – I didn't care, it just had to be something
I had never experienced before.

During these 100 days, a close friend of mine handed me a book
called *The Power of Habit*. He didn't hand me this book because I was a
book reader. In all honesty, the last book I had fully read prior to the
one being gifted to me was *Green Eggs and Ham* by Dr. Suess - and I'm
not kidding. All through school, I used SparkNotes and other online
book summary sites to get by. Thankfully the universe placed this book
(*The Power of Habit*) in my hands at a time when I was **willing** to do
things I usually wouldn't – and so I read it. This book brought a harsh
truth to my attention: *we're all living our lives, walking around doing
things that we're not entirely conscious of, without even questioning it.* The
power in this truth is that **our lives are mainly shaped by the things
we do without thinking; because more of our time is spent doing
those things, rather than the things we know we want to do**. This
is why someone can WANT to be the kind of person who wakes up
earlier, yet they'll have 9 different alarms set for the morning and

snooze each of them. The snoozing is the habit; so their life becomes waking up and doing exactly that. That was me for a long time, but in almost every area of my life, especially food. I realized I was eating the same things over and over again, without thinking or questioning why. Eating healthier became something I wanted to tap into. Keep in mind this all stemmed from me being sick of the way life was turning out for me.

A few months after finishing the first book I had read in full since childhood, that same friend who gifted me the book also recommended that I watch a documentary called *Forks Over Knives*. The documentary was kind of old-fashioned and not the most exciting thing to watch, but my being in a place of <u>wanting to do anything involving flipping my life upside down</u> was enough to push through the whole thing. I could not be more serious, nor more passionate, in saying that documentary shifted my way of thinking about food. I now had even more reason to change my life. **I watched doctors reverse diseases that I have witnessed, firsthand, take the lives of countless family members and people in general. Those diseases were cancer and diabetes. Prior to this documentary, I had accepted and wholeheartedly believed that diseases like these were hereditary, and just part of life in an uncontrollable way.** I believed that medicine and chemotherapy were the ONLY ways to fight these diseases, which were already incurable. I was also young, and believed that I wouldn't have to worry about diseases like cancer and diabetes until I was older – after all, I had only seen older family members die from these illnesses. Then life punched my family and I in the throat harder than usual: we lost a 9-year-old to cancer - which leads me into the next segment.

Why I stay vegan

Anyone who comes to me expressing interest in going vegan has always heard the same response: *"That is awesome! I love your reason, and if you're going to stick with it, you're also going to need a **special reason.**"*

I say this because we are creatures of habit; so when we get spurts of new motivation, eventually it wears off, and who we are at our core comes back out to play. A 'special reason' is something that shakes you at your core; it's enough to change who you are. You see, wanting to go vegan because you watched a documentary that exposed the murder of innocent baby chicks and cute cows is enough for some, but very few. Wanting to go vegan because of some newly acquired information that you can relate to is enough for some, but very few. New motivation eventually wears off and is never there when you truly need it. New motivation, for most, won't be enough to push back against a way of eating that has been established for decades. And most importantly, **going vegan and staying vegan are two different beasts**.

Losing my 9-year-old cousin shook me at my core. It taught me that **young age does not mean invincibility**. It shifted my thinking from "I'll eat healthier later on in life" to "I need to take my eating seriously now". That experience changed everything for me. It put things into perspective in a way I had not before. Suddenly I realized that not only had I spent a major portion of my teenage years and early 20s in the hospital watching family members suffer and die from things like cancer, heart disease, and diabetes, but now I've also watched my Aunt have to witness, firsthand, watching her son slowly be eaten away by a disease that is far too normalized by society. **This period of time was challenging because everything I knew to be true was being challenged. And I finally realized that <u>one of the most common things we do as humans is pray for/want a life that is inconsistent with our choices and habits</u>**. I've personally sat on my knees and prayed for family to be spared from diseases that are, in part, a result of the foods those same family members were eating. I've watched hospitals feed patients foods that have science-backed studies linked to the diseases they were treating; I saw this happen with my cousin during his final days. One of the most profound ways I've heard this inconsistency summarized is in a quote that goes: *"It is amazing how little attention the food industry pays to health, and how little attention the health industry pays to food."*

The culmination of these things led me to 2 decisions:

1. I am not going to poison myself with the very same foods my family has been eating for decades.
2. I am not going to be responsible for my kids (although I don't have any yet) spending their youth watching me rot in the hospital from diseases that we can actually avoid by making healthier eating choices.

My reason for going vegan is health. My special reason for staying vegan is my cousin, Zechariah Elijah. I dedicate my journey down the path of food choices to him.

I do acknowledge that I can still die at any given point and time from an overwhelming list of things, **but I do not use that as an excuse to be lazy in my choices** today, nor as an excuse to be unintentionally ignorant to the pain I may cause for people who care about me, by having to watch me rot in a hospital bed from food-related illnesses that I can influence. There's not much nobility in that. **If I know better, I've got to do better - because my choices don't just affect me, they affect people I may not have even met yet. And yes, the same goes for you.**

The Benefit

I lied. There's a few. Lets dive in! Allow me to lighten the mood by confessing a truth that just isn't talked about too frequently: *my poops are incredible.* Don't be jealous. Look, it's been 4 years since I've suffered from constipation or diarrhea in the slightest bit! I understand that I won't receive a gold medal for this, but I want you to experience this kind of ease and flow in your life. It may not be guaranteed that your body will respond the same way, but is that not something worth striving for?

On a more serious note, as for my personal benefits, there's a wide range. But there is this one in particular that stands out - that would be... **my *being***. I don't mean to get all deep and spiritual on you, but I will at the expense of giving you the truth. The awakening that has happened within who I am at my core has been insanely profound and refreshing. As I mentioned earlier, I went vegan for the health benefits. I ended up extracting so much more from this change. My connection to self, the universe & it's energies, and all living beings & creatures has stretched farther than everything that *I was* prior. **Whether direct or indirect, making a positive and unfamiliar change in what foods I consume daily has enabled me to love deeper, understand more, react less, see clearer, feel more, create more, elevate consciousness, and levitate**. Okay so I haven't really levitated but I am working on it. My point is that this **one change in one area of my life** was the genesis of a domino effect that has allowed me access to doors that the old version of me would never have seen, because **the old version of me was not looking**. If there is one thing I have learned in this life, it is that IF YOU WANT OPPORTUNITY & CHANGE, YOU MUST GO LOOK FOR IT FIRST. I'm still amazed at all the things I find in the grocery store, that have been there all along, but I never saw because I wasn't looking. **The same goes for what lies on the shelves in the aisles of life. If you keep walking in and doing all of your shopping in aisle 2,3,4 and 5 - you'll never know what aisle 10 has to offer.**

Why You Should Try It & What To Expect

I once heard this quote that has stuck with me ever since: *"Living food for the living body."* It resonated so deeply because I eventually grew to translate it into "Living food for the living life". It's a slight remix but hear me out... One of the greatest fascinations of my life has presented itself in the form of the following statement: **I am perpetually amazed and utterly shocked at the irony of people wanting a LIVELY & VIBRANT life, yet eating DEAD animals.** Don't run from this chapter yet, I promise I'm not being judgmental. I'll actually go as far as saying that it's incredibly easy for me to make that statement in hindsight. I was once doing that EXACT thing - **living a life that was not in harmony with the one I was praying for.**

This is my 1st recommended reason for trying a vegan diet - **you're a living being, so it doesn't seem far-fetched to assume that the consumption of living foods are better suited for your body, mind, and soul, than dead foods.** If the law of attraction in it's simplest form suggests that you attract what you are...and you are what you eat...it also doesn't seem far-fetched to eat living foods so that you attract a living and vibrant life.

My 2nd recommended reason is one of awareness of morality, which like most things of the human experience, is completely subjective & up to you. **I simply encourage you to ask yourself if your moral compass (meaning what you consider acceptable and unacceptable) is consistent, or if it has been shaped by the environment you were raised in.** One of the most common inconsistencies in morality presents itself in the form of **value of life.** Allow me to explain... The average person probably agrees that taking a new born baby from it's parents and killing it is wrong, yet this is *precisely* what we do to animals. The average person probably also agrees that slaughtering animals is wrong and that it should be done humanely if required, yet most of us would not voluntarily submit our dog, cat, or house-pet for a 'humane' death on any given day. Consider for a moment the underlying principal of these examples, and you will find that **our minds have mainly been conditioned to see things in ways favorable to ourselves.** Does it not seem a bit weird to NOT want animals to be slaughtered, yet still eat animals for breakfast, lunch, and dinner?

This is not a matter of right or wrong; that's completely up to you. This is a matter of being more efficient. Oxford defines *efficient* as "achieving maximum productivity...preventing the wasteful use of a particular resource." **One of our greatest resources are our minds. I simply ask that we be aware of what we choose to view as moral and immoral, and reflect on our own actions.** That is all. Also go vegan, yes, but that too is up to you.

My 3rd recommended reason is very much immaterial. **Do it because it is far from who you currently are. Try it because it's unfamiliar. Try it because you're currently comfortable and all too familiar with what you eat now. Try it as a means of EXPANDING YOURSELF. Try it out of sheer curiosity; and if you're not at all curious about a vegan lifestyle, try it for the simple fact that in order to face yourself...you must break the current version of you.** (See chapter titled *"How to Face Yourself"*)

This is bigger than just "feeling better" or "more energized". Yes, those are a few benefits, but it's more so about WHAT YOU CAN DO & THE LIFE YOU MANIFEST WHEN YOU FEEL YOUR BEST AND ARE MORE ENERGIZED. This is for the sake of exploring outside the lines that you have created for yourself. You DESERVE to lead a healthy and wealthy life. You DESERVE to LEARN new things about food and the replacements for things you currently love. **You have the elasticity to bend beyond what you currently know, and still be okay**!

You will not die of veganism, I promise you. Beyond my reasons for trying it, there lie many more that I can not share with you because they are YOURS to uncover. You'll run into so many more reasons and benefits that are unique to you and your life.

Ultimately, you will have explored YOU as a person and taken on a new opportunity. 30, 60, 90 days... 1 year. Whatever works for you! Just keep in mind how long you have NOT been vegan, and give yourself a fair chance to go head to head with that amount of time. All too often, I see people give up after a few days - try not to do that. **Your effort should be in direct proportion to your desire to live a more fulfilling life**! I say all of this with love, and remember it's my plea - not a command, nor an attack on your character.

As for what to expect - a change. Your body WILL respond in some way, be prepared for that and create time for research to do it efficiently. I have heard of many different initial reactions by the body - these are mostly responses from our body to a huge change, not you dying. And no, it's not more expensive (definitely doesn't have to be); that's a myth. We have mainly been conditioned to pay for cheap food. Don't be afraid to Google "how to go vegan on a budget" if you need. Go have some fun with it!

DO IT BECAUSE IT IS FAR FROM WHO YOU CURRENTLY ARE. TRY IT BECAUSE IT'S UNFAMILIAR. TRY IT BECAUSE YOU'RE CURRENTLY COMFORTABLE AND ALL TOO FAMILIAR WITH WHAT YOU EAT NOW. TRY IT AS A MEANS OF EXPANDING YOURSELF. TRY IT OUT OF SHEER CURIOSITY; AND IF YOU'RE NOT AT ALL CURIOUS ABOUT A VEGAN LIFESTYLE, TRY IT FOR THE SIMPLE FACT THAT IN ORDER TO FACE YOURSELF...YOU MUST BREAK THE CURRENT VERSION OF YOU.

31

How You Can Save/Change the World

I t's not at all coincidence that this chapter is being written during an emotionally pressing time for the world. Currently, a major portion of the world is mourning the death of a man who died at the hands of another, via an 8+ minute torturous act. **This event happens to be an undesirable reflection of just one of the many things we're still working on getting right as human beings.** In the midst of chaos, loud noises, climatic emotions, provoking opinions, one-sided narratives, and everything aforementioned being excessively perpetuated by a world of media that is now more influential than ever…yes, it becomes more and more enticing to join the conversation and assume the emotional burden that comes with it. **If you're genuinely a good person, or an empath, you'll especially feel an emotional responsibility to do something about what is going on around you.**

In this book, we don't believe in 'problems' - we consider those to be *opportunities to heal and improve.* One of the first and most important things to realize about these *opportunities* is that they are not likely to heal and improve by one single act or event - this is step 1. Step 2 is to embrace the fact that the bulk of these *opportunities* are, in sum, created by us. (Us meaning human beings, and who we are internally at our core.) An important, underlying aspect to this step is understanding that **embracing responsibility** (not fault) **to heal and improve damages in our way of life, simultaneously means putting an end to finger-pointing** (fault). Step 3 is to listen, and listen solely to understand, not to agree or respond. This is the ultimate sacrifice; and I can guarantee that you will not receive a gold medal of acknowledgement for this. You'll receive more - wisdom, knowledge, understanding, and compassion. **'Problems' scale as a result of a lacking in wisdom, knowledge, understanding, and compassion by all parties involved. Solutions occur as a byproduct of actively & intentionally seeking out wisdom, knowledge, understanding, and compassion**. Please note that *agreement* is nowhere to be found in these steps. Seeking out understanding, even when unaccompanied by agreement, is where healing and improving begin.

Step 3, in short, is shutting up...even when you know you're right...even when the other person is dead wrong...even when you disagree...even when you are in utter shock of the stupidity of another...and even when you can justifiably speak your opinion and communicate your emotions. Replace the ease of speaking up and potentially "spazzing out" (even when you know you're right) with seeking to understand instead. Take heed to the following: **seeking to understand has no end, and that's the point - if all parties embrace the opportunity to be in an ongoing state of desiring more of an understanding of others and their views (even in the face of disagreement), the mood of the conversation changes - ultimately changing our actions (because we tend to act out mood).** Now the conversation shifts to everyone being heard. It is from here, that solutions may be birthed.

Step 4 lies just on the other side of the former: it is being a good person. Yes, this is in some ways an oversimplification, but not in all. Hear me out… **Something incredible happens when we accept that change is not an event (but a manifestation of choices over time), embrace responsibility, and seek understanding - we, free of resistance and ego, tap into what our contribution to the world looks like. This is how you save/change the world.**

Rather than allowing yourself to be distracted by the shiny objects that present themselves in the form of loud noises, debates, riots, finger-pointing, protests, ego-driven communication, and media consumption…you, instead, change the conversation via your being an active force in the direction of good. Realizing that **who you are is what you bring to the world,** in the same breath, allows for furthering the importance of **PRIORITIZING WHO YOU ARE.** When we do this at scale, the world changes. Bringing anything less than the best version of ourselves to the world, only perpetuates the world's ~~problems~~ *opportunities* to heal and improve.

1. **Accept that change requires a manifestation of choices over time, not an event.**
2. **Embrace responsibility, not fault.**
3. **Listen. To seek understanding.**
4. **Be a good person/Prioritize who you are (what you bring to the world)**

IF YOU'RE GENUINELY A GOOD PERSON, OR AN EMPATH, YOU'LL ESPECIALLY FEEL AN EMOTIONAL RESPONSIBILITY TO DO SOMETHING ABOUT WHAT IS GOING ON AROUND YOU.

32

Putting This All Together

I am not going to lie to you. This is not going to be easy. 'This' meaning transforming yourself into the kind of person who experiences fulfillment in every single area of your life while being contagiously-gold. Creating the life you desire is far from a snap of the finger away. It also doesn't lie on the other side of a single meditation session. I don't want you to try to change things over the next 30 days. Not even over the next year. Let go of 'time'. Rather, **what to do from here is dedicate the entirety of your life to exploring how infinitely incredible you can be.** Take the principles from each chapter of this book and harmonize who you are at your core with them. Be a student of everything that stimulates some sort of emotion within you, especially if it's fear or uncertainty. More importantly, be a student of you, and REMAIN that.

How far the magnitude of your fulfillment and experience of life go, will greatly depend on how far the magnitude of your self-exploration go. [Read that once more.] Give yourself permission right now to let go of all material desired outcomes. They are all false summits. What no one else is telling you is that there are no summits! When you climb the ladder of self-exploration, you will eventually end up going further and further and further and further and further and further and further and...you get the point. Rather than try to get your body to look like Cristiano Rinaldo's or Kylie Jenner's or [insert some other person with a great body], simply BE the kind of person who goes to the gym or works out daily; THE BYPRODUCT WILL BE the amazing body you develop. Rather than try to get married by a certain age, simply BE the kind of person who is *whole* and fully emerged in self-love; THE BYPRODUCT WILL BE the soulmate you attract while on **your own** journey. Rather than aiming to have things 'figured out' by a certain age, simply BE the kind of person who is constantly feeding themselves knowledge; THE BY PRODUCT WILL BE the overwhelming amount of things you figure out! Rather than want to be rich, simply BE the kind of person who studies the habits of the wealthy and applies the principles; THE BYPRODUCT WILL BE the money you begin to amass. In sum, **life is going to reflect the kind of person you are**.

Your desired outcome is most efficient when it is rooted in internal shifts of being. Because who you are within, shapes the life you create externally. So, what now? Well, YOU. Start with a shift of focus from all things external, like your job, whether your're single or not, how much money you have or don't have, how far you have to go, how much you've accomplished, how bad your past has been, how much your boss sucks, how you're not where you want to be yet, how much the odds are stacked against you in your environment, how your circumstances are undesirable, blah blah blah. **Circumstance and all of these THINGS outside of who you are at your core, are a distraction from you shaping your being to reflect a fulfilling experience of life.** Don't be distracted by the 'things' - they're all made up by other people. Even completing this book is a 'thing'. Things are cool, but not what you want to shape your identity behind. Let your identity be the lead, and all the *things* will follow. YOU created the time to complete this book (internal), and the byproduct is your completing this book (external thing). **The strength, confidence, and core of your identity need be in nothing else but the depth of your self-exploration.**

When we build our identity around accomplishments, things we've done, things we haven't, failures & successes, how much we have or don't have, image & appearance, likes & followers, and other external factors...we become susceptible to destruction of the very identity we built; this is because in order for that type of identity to stand tall, other things, that are mainly uncontrollable, must also stand tall. When those things are lacking, our identity then falls. **When our identity is built around one fundamental controllable -** *exploration of infinite self* **- in the face of any and all circumstance, WE BECOME INDESTRUCTIBLE AND BULLETPROOF. Even more, we become fulfilled, and when we operate from a place of fulfillment...we are contagiously-gold. THAT MEANS ANYTHING AND EVERYTHING YOU TOUCH TURNS TO GOLD (YOUR LIFE INCLUDED), AS A BYPRODUCT OF WHO YOU ARE.**

WHEN OUR IDENTITY IS BUILT AROUND ONE FUNDAMENTAL CONTROLLABLE – EXPLORATION OF INFINITE SELF – IN THE FACE OF ANY AND ALL CIRCUMSTANCE, WE BECOME INDESTRUCTIBLE AND BULLETPROOF. EVEN MORE, WE BECOME FULFILLED, AND WHEN WE OPERATE FROM A PLACE OF FULFILLMENT... WE ARE CONTAGIOUSLY– GOLD.

Closing Remarks

Look, I know could have just placed what I'm about to say in the previous chapter, but I thought it was kind of cool to have a "closing remarks" section. I feel fancier. You've made it this far, so I'll keep this brief.

Come back to the principles within this book from time to time. Hell, read it all over again if you want. I promise you there is no rule book anywhere stating that you can not start this book from the beginning tomorrow. I know it's kind of cliche to say, but apply everything you've learned in these pages. Even further, harmonize your being with them. Mold these principles into your DNA. In my perfect world, you wouldn't even have to come back to this book after a while... You would just BECOME everything you've learned here. You are going to operate from a place that reflects every second you have invested into yourself while reading this.

Gift this book to a friend that you know could use it, or just tell them about it and threaten them with 19 years of bad luck if they don't buy it and read it in it's entirety. I'm just kidding, but if you want to do that, I 100% support you. **On a more serious note, spread the magic of this book via the #inameditchallenge - simply post a video stating "I named it", what *"contagiously-gold"* means to you, and nominate 2 people to get this book and read it as well** - using the hashtag #inameditchallenge.

If you have not yet written out your own affirmations, or need a little help with some daily vibes to speak into yourself, feel free to look up

"The Affirmation Booklet" - a pocket-sized book made specifically for you to read aloud daily - and it takes about a 5 minutes to read. It's the perfect way to kick-start your day, or to just read whenever you need a boost.

Lastly, be sure to follow @younameitbook on Instagram, and check out and join our Facebook group *"You Name It Community"* - a community for people like yourself, who have completed this book, and want to connect with like-minded individuals who are also on their growth path. It's the perfect place to mastermind. Make sure to post "I named it!" and your biggest takeaway(s) from the book so that the other members can easily connect with you. You can build a whole new additional group of friends there! And if you're feeling extra hungry and want to catapult your self-development, email me directly at younameit@infiniteco.us - where we can discuss 1-on-1 coaching, or simply coming up with a plan to set your footsteps in the most efficient direction from here.

Lastly pt2 - I know that this may seem like a lot to ask, but I definitely recommend you write a book report on what you learned from this book. This is a tactic I personally do after each book I finish reading, and the benefits have been powerful. Maybe it's been years since you've done a book report, and that's okay. There are no rules for this one. No minimum amount of pages or anything like that. I just want you to have something to come back to whenever you need. Fill it up with your biggest takeaways. The best part is that by writing this book report, you're going to help yourself retain a lot more information.

My Book Recommendations

- *The Miracle Morning: The Not-So-Obvious Secret Guaranteed to Transform Your Life (Before 8am)* by Hal Elrod
- *The Four Agreements: A Practical Guide to Personal Freedom* by

Don Miguel Ruiz
- *Rich Dad Poor Dad* by Robert Kiyosaki
- *The Power of Habit* by Charles Duhigg
- *Think and Grow Rich* by Napoleon Hill
- *Limitless: Upgrade Your Brain, Learn Anything Faster, and Unlock Your Exceptional Life* by Jim Kwik
- *Man's Search for Meaning* by Viktor E. Frankl
- *The 10x Rule* by Grant Cardone
- *The Affirmation Booklet* by Tarik Trotter

My Movie Recommendations

- *Me and Earl and The Dying Girl*
- *Good Will Hunting*
- *Interstellar*
- *The Life of Pi*
- *Inside Out* (Disney)
- *The Secret Life of Walter Mitty*
- *Arrival*
- *Awakenings*
- *The Current Wars*

About the Author

Tarik Trotter is a professional recording artist and songwriter with over a decade of experience in the music industry. Tarik's voluminous writing background shines through his newest 1-2 combo of hard-hitting self-help books: *"You Name It"* and *"The Affirmation Booklet"*. He is a student of life and has spent the last five years studying the likes of exceptional individuals who rose from unfavorable circumstances. Tarik has traveled extensively through mental, emotional, and spiritual depths of self – with the purpose of discovering the infinite supply we hold within, so that he may help others do the same. Tarik is now focusing on multiple projects, most notably his charity foundation – Infinite Collective Foundation – which has a mission of raising contagiously-gold generations, providing a safe haven for children all over the world, and watering the 100 years that follow our own.

You can connect with me on:
- 𝕏 https://twitter.com/tariktrotter
- 📘 https://www.facebook.com/tariktrotter
- 🔗 https://www.instagram.com/tariktrotter

Also by Tarik Trotter

It's currently mid-2020 and I'm super early into my career as an author. Having a 10 year + ongoing music career as a songwriter and professional recording artist, there's thankfully been some skill-overflow into being an author. Whether it be in music or book form, you'll find my content to mainly assume the role of empowering self. I like to create theme-music for the superhero within you. With a passionate belief in our being infinite within, I am on a mission to help as many as possible explore just how much we are capable of.

The Affirmation Booklet

A pocket-sized book made specifically for you to read aloud to yourself daily - and it only takes about 5 minutes to read. It's the perfect way to kick-start your day, or to just read whenever in need of a boost. Enjoy this booklet full of words for confidence, health, happiness, relationships, creativity, finances, career, and more!

Made in the USA
San Bernardino, CA
14 August 2020

77049123R00136